STEVE McQUEEN

The Final Chapter

STEVE McQUEEN

The Final Chapter

GRADY RAGSDALE JR.

Vision House
A Division of GL Publications
Ventura, CA U.S.A.

© Copyright 1983 by Grady Ragsdale, Jr.
All rights reserved

Published by Vision House Inc.
A Division of GL Publications
Ventura, California 93006

Library of Congress Cataloging in Publication data

Ragsdale, Grady, 1946-
    Steve McQueen, the final chapter.

    1. McQueen, Steve 1930-   . 2. Moving-picture actors and actresses—
United States—Biography.
I. Title.
PN2287.M19R33   1983   791.43'028'0924 [B]   83-14681
ISBN 0-88449-105-6

For Steve and Barbara

ACKNOWLEDGMENTS

Thanks to God for His inspiration in the lives of those who made this story possible, and for enabling me to tell the story the way Steve would have it told.

My thanks and love to my beautiful wife Judy Marie Ragsdale for her understanding, and as my co-writer and typist in helping me produce this book, and my dearest love to my two daughters Tami and Erica.

My sincere thanks to my dearest friend Barbara McQueen for her contributing help in editing and approving this book. Her complimentary remarks, "It is a sweet, terrific, and dignified book. You did well by Steve. Steve would have liked it because it shows a different side of him other than the motorcycles and race cars."

My thanks to Doctor Billy Graham for his friendship and sharing his spiritual experience and encouragement during Steve's final hours.

Thanks to Sammy Mason for introducing me to Steve and sharing his experience about Steve as a fellow pilot and Christian.

My thanks to my dear friend and Christian John Daly for sharing his personal and spiritual relationship with Steve.

My special thanks to Clete Roberts for twenty-five years of friendship and for encouraging me and insisting that I write this book.

Grady Ragsdale, Jr.

FOREWORD

Steve McQueen was an American original, a tough guy
with a troubled past who touched the rebel in each of us.
He tended to be a loner, quiet and introspective. He
respected the privacy of others and expected them to
treat him in the same way. His life changed dramatically
over the years. He rose from maverick to superstar—and
legend. On screen, he was almost invincible. Off screen,
almost wasn't nearly good enough.

During the uncertain summer of 1980, as Steve
McQueen lay in his hospital bed, he talked of writing a
book. It was to be more than the story of his courageous
fight against cancer, and the program he so truly believed
was helping win that fight. It was to be a reflection of his
new life, one filled with hope and a faith reborn.

Steve McQueen's interest in spiritual things first came

to my attention through an article in the press. It was next brought to my attention by Bill Brown, president of World Wide Pictures in Burbank. Bill also told me that Steve wanted to see me, but no definite date was set.

In September 1980 I was in Hawaii and about to go for several weeks of meetings in Japan when Bill Brown rather urgently called me, saying that Steve McQueen really wanted to see me, or at least talk to me over the telephone. He gave me several numbers. I called them all before I finally got in contact with Grady Ragsdale. I told Grady that I heard Steve wanted to get in touch with me. Steve was in Mexico, Grady said, but he would tell him that I had called.

After I returned home from Japan I called Grady's home and talked with his wife, Judy. She said that Grady was at Steve's ranch and she would have him return my call. When he did he asked if I would come to Santa Paula to see Steve.

I look back on that experience with thanksgiving and some amazement. I had planned to minister to Steve, but as it turned out, he ministered to me. I saw once again the reality of what Jesus Christ can do for a man in his last hours. It was also interesting to me that Steve had accepted Christ some weeks before he even knew he was ill. Otherwise people might have thought it was a deathbed decision.

Grady Ragsdale was not only Steve McQueen's trusted, devoted friend but also his companion and confidant. Their friendship began with a mutual interest in flying. It ended with a love of life.

The Final Chapter is Grady Ragsdale's tribute to Steve McQueen. It is also a portrait of a man few people knew and understood.

Billy Graham

STEVE McQUEEN

The Final Chapter

Chapter One

The southbound freeway through the San Fernando Valley was jammed with holiday traffic. For the past hour, since leaving the quiet town of Santa Paula some sixty miles north, the roadway had been virtually clear. Now, approaching the sprawling city, I sat red-faced in the reflected glow of brake lights. It was a different world.

I watched the traffic inch forward, slowly angling toward the off-ramps that led to the mammoth malls and shopping centers. Below, on the streets, drivers vied for parking places beneath garlands of glitter. I envied them their moment of spirited, seasonal panic. But on that early evening of December 23 in 1979, shopping was the last thing on my mind. For the first time in my life Christmas seemed unimportant. I'd left the tranquility of Santa Paula behind with just a single thought: helping a friend through a tough time.

I remained on the southbound freeway until it connected with another, this one leading eastward toward Hollywood. Then I was on a narrow, winding road cutting across the mountainous barrier that divided the valley from the great basin. The Dodge van took the hairpin curves in stride. Still I felt uneasy carrying such precious cargo, carton upon carton of gaily wrapped and ribboned boxes, presents purchased before the shocking discovery earlier in the week. I had no idea what the boxes contained, or their value. But I was determined that they reach their destination undamaged.

At last I was on the flatlands again, traveling along Beverly Boulevard, and as I passed La Cienega it came into view: the towering walls of the multi-winged Cedars-Sinai Medical Center. My eyes traveled upward searching out the eighth floor. Somewhere behind the endless grid of glowing windows lay the man who called himself Don Schoonover. It was a name to remember, a name that would admit me past the guarded entry to his room. But it was not the name that I, and the world, knew so well. That could not be spoken without endangering a special trust. If anyone were to ask, Don Schoonover was the patient in question. Don Schoonover, not Steve McQueen.

It was impossible to picture Steve in that sterile setting; white upon white, sleek and uncluttered and ultra-modern. He belonged on his ranch, in his home filled with memorabilia of the past, with his presents clustered about the Christmas tree that fairly sagged with colorful antique ornaments. He belonged in Santa Paula, not in a strange hospital room. "For the first time in my life," Steve had told me only weeks earlier, "everything's beautiful. I used to be running away, now I'm running toward something. My roots. And, man, am I happy!"

Santa Paula was about as far away from Hollywood as Steve could get—in spirit. Set within the fertile Santa

Clara River Valley, surrounded by lush groves of orange, lemon, walnut, and avocado trees and gently rolling hillsides, the atmosphere is serene and friendly. It is a small town, a community of approximately twenty thousand people.

Despite attempts at modernization, the lingering effect is rural Americana. Hitching posts still line the city streets and a barn-like general store, built in the 1880s, continues to be a popular mercantile center. A museum, housed in picturesque turn-of-the-century quarters near the business district, displays historic items of local interest.

Only fourteen miles inland from the Pacific Ocean, Santa Paula boasts a mild Mediterranean climate that attracts visitors. And it has an airport, a small privately owned facility that is "home base" for over 300 aircraft and nearly 600 pilots. That, at first, was the big lure for Steve McQueen.

Steve began coming to the airport in the early part of 1979, shortly after completing his role in the film *Tom Horn*, in the hope of buying a plane. He wanted to learn how to fly. I didn't meet Steve then—and I wouldn't for several months—but I learned about those early visits from the few people he'd met at the time and, later, from Steve himself.

As Steve remembered, "I'd driven up from Malibu with my girl friend, Barbara Minty. There weren't many people around at the time so we did some walking. Finally, we found an open hangar and we looked inside. All we could see was a restored Apache airplane. No people, no activity. I didn't want to interrupt anything so I asked if we could come in, just in case."

From behind the plane, Steve recalled, came an answer. "Sure, make yourself at home," the voice said. A moment later a coverall-clad man in his fifties appeared smiling as he introduced himself. His name was Perry

Schreffler. He was a pilot of long-standing, over thirty years service, with Trans World Airlines.

"I didn't think he'd recognized me with my scruffy beard," Steve said, "so I gave him my name. Then I introduced Barbara." (Perry later admitted he knew the identity of his visitor immediately. Beard or not, there was no mistaking Steve McQueen.)

Steve told Perry Schreffler what he was up to, that he had come to the airport in search of a Stearman open cockpit biplane, a Boeing model of the type he had owned years before but never had the chance to fly. A friend had wrecked it, he said, and now he was in the market for another Stearman, as well as a good flight instructor.

"Perry disappeared for a second," Steve explained, "and returned with a copy of a flying magazine that had listings of planes for sale and trade. For the next hour we concentrated on the Stearman ads. If I found one to my liking Perry would offer guidance not only on prices but on general conditions, like flying time indicated on engines and airframes. Before Barbara and I left Perry's hangar that day I had a lead on a plane offered by a company in Missouri specializing in Stearman restorations." He was also told about a man named Sammy Mason.

"Sammy's one of the finest Stearman pilots in the country bar none," Perry told Steve, "and he's based here in Santa Paula. With a little convincing I'm sure he'd be your instructor."

Forty-eight hours later Steve was on the phone with Perry Schreffler, bringing him up to date. Steve had been busy. Not only had he ordered a mint condition 1943 Stearman biplane from the Missouri company but he'd called Sammy Mason.

"Perry was full of questions," Steve remembered. Then, with a grin, he added, "I put him on, but not by much. That go-around with Sammy Mason was rough."

Sammy had told Steve that he wasn't interested in taking on new primary students, only those with advanced training, particularly aerobatics.

Steve wouldn't take no for an answer. "I told Sammy how much I wanted to learn to fly—old planes, not modern ones—and that I definitely wanted and *needed* him to teach me. Sammy said he might be able to find another instructor but I told him that wouldn't do. I wanted *him*. Well, we went back and forth for some time and I think he got a little fed up with me because he said there wasn't any use discussing it further. He couldn't even fit me into his schedule." The conversation ended with Sammy having the final say. But Steve called him back, not once but twice. At last Sammy agreed to meet with Steve at the airport where they could discuss Steve's dilemma face to face. As Steve put it, beaming with a sense of accomplishment, "We got together and worked everything out."

Sammy Mason was no pushover for Steve McQueen. At six feet tall, with a halo of snow white hair and bushy white eyebrows, Sammy is an imposing figure. He was then in his early sixties, and had been retired from Lockheed for five years following a distinguished career as an engineering test pilot. Sammy was enjoying his new freedom, one that permitted selectivity in his scheduling. At this point in his life he didn't need an eager novice for a student.

Later, Sammy Mason told me about that eventful meeting: "Although Steve was persistent, the tone of his voice was kindly and I couldn't really get angry with him. However, I figured that my stubbornness was at least equal to Steve McQueen's—until I stood facing him. Anyone who ever met Steve will testify to his extremely magnetic personality. An instant friendship was permanently welded the moment we got together. The fact that he was a movie star didn't occupy a significant part of my feelings toward him. Steve didn't want undue attention; he just wanted to fit in with the other pilots in the airport."

Steve was now rarin' to fly. The Stearman he had ordered had yet to arrive but that didn't hold him back. On March 15, 1979, in a borrowed 1940 Stearman biplane, he began his training.

According to Sammy, Steve was an excellent student. "He had an exceptional aptitude for flying, and he possessed considerable natural flying talent and coordination. And he was fun to work with, tremendously enthusiastic. In the cockpit, Steve was a nearly inexhaustible source of energy, able to take several consecutive hours of instruction without any indication of declining attention or fatigue.

"But there were times too, I knew, when Steve would suddenly tire, generally nearing the end of a particularly strenuous day's activity. In untypical fashion, he would exclaim without warning, 'Let's quit, I'm exhausted.' "

Steve appeared to be especially cautious at this stage of his training, Sammy said. He took flying seriously and approached his introduction to it with great respect. Steve refused to push himself or risk taking chances as he had done so often in the past racing cars and dirt bikes.

The airport soon became a second home for Steve, much as it had been for me. I'd done some flying myself; it was my livelihood, originally as a cropduster, most recently as a helicopter pilot. Then, in January of 1979 I suffered a mild heart attack. A heart attack at the ripe old age of 32! Doctors blamed it on the pesticides used in spraying. I wasn't convinced but it didn't make any difference. Right or wrong, from that day on I was grounded. I continued to work around the airport, however, mainly for veteran newscaster Clete Roberts. Clete, a weekend flyer, was one of the airport's old guards. I had known him for over twenty years; he was like a father to me.

One day in April, as I drove past Sammy Mason's

hangar, I noticed a yellow Stearman parked in front. It was a plane I had never seen before so I stopped to take a closer look. Then I saw Sammy. He was with another man; they were trying to fish an object from the bottom of the fuselage with a broom handle. I stood by until they pulled out the culprit—a ball-point pen. When they turned around, Sammy introduced me to his friend.

It wasn't really necessary. Even in faded jeans and a soiled T-shirt, bearded and his blond hair long and flecked with gray, I recognized him. The clear blue eyes were definitely Steve McQueen's.

Steve McQueen had long been a favorite of mine. As a youngster I'd watched him in his television series *Wanted—Dead or Alive.* Most of his movies were ones I'd seen, and I knew of his fascination with machinery and racing. I also knew of his need for privacy. I tried to respect that.

Steve offered his hand and I took it, expecting a grip that was in keeping with his screen image: strong and masculine. What I felt instead was weak and limp. As I soon discovered, Steve was highly suspicious of all newcomers—and shaking hands was his first test when meeting someone. By offering a light grip he felt he could better judge a person or, as he put it, "absorb the vibrations." And the vibrations had better be positive!

I squeezed, but lightly, almost fearful I would break his hand.

I must have passed Steve's test for he was friendly from the start. We talked briefly about planes, mainly his new Stearman, and as we walked around the aircraft he pointed with great pride to its many features. He was like a child with a long-awaited new toy.

The arrival of the plane created a problem, however. He had no place to store it. Leaving it outside exposed to the elements and strangers did not sit well with him.

Over the next few weeks Steve and I saw one another only now and again. We waved but didn't speak. But as I worked about the airport I followed his progress in flight training. He was now preparing for his first solo flight, flying in tandem with Sammy's son, Pete Mason, a highly skilled pilot in his own right.

On May 1, following a series of takeoffs and landings, Pete stepped from the cockpit leaving Steve alone inside. Without hesitating, Steve taxied the plane to the end of the runway where he pushed the throttle to the wall. Moments later he was airborne, circling over the airport in a basic flight pattern until he was properly lined up for the final approach—and a perfect three-point landing. The exercise lasted only minutes, but from Steve's expression it was long enough for the thrill of a lifetime.

Not long after Steve's first solo flight a 1931 Pitcairn Mailwing biplane flew into the airport. It was a magnificent restoration of an early airmail machine with a large 420-horsepower Wright whirlwind engine mounted on the nose. The plane immediately caught Steve's attention— he had seen photos of it in a flying magazine—and he took off to talk with the owner who made it clear from the start that he had no intention of selling.

The following morning I saw Steve standing outside Sammy Mason's hangar. "Come here, Grady," he hollered, "I want to show you something." He took me inside and there was the Pitcairn. "It's mine," he beamed. "I got it for $65,000."

By mid-month, Steve had a hangar of his own in a choice spot, set off from the others at the east end of the airport. He had made the previous owner an offer the man couldn't refuse.

Steve's prized planes now had a home, but before they were moved the hangar had to be completely cleaned, inside and out. That done, he hired a crew to install a fully-equipped kitchen, bath and shower, and a small side room paneled in cedar where he put an old-fashioned potbellied stove.

A few weeks later Steve called me into his hangar to see the completed remodeling. On our way through the kitchen area he pulled two beers from the refrigerator. Handing me one, he said, "How would you like to work for me?"

I didn't know what Steve had in mind but it turned out he was talking about a full-time job, and the pay was excellent. Lately, work had been sporadic. I was tempted.

"You probably don't know this," Steve said, "but I had you checked out. I have all my employees checked out before they work for me. I have to be able to trust people. When there's trust you can relax." He reached in his pocket, pulled out a pack of Apple Jack chewing tobacco, and offered me a hunk. I refused, lighting a cigarette instead. He looked at me oddly as he placed a wad of tobacco in his mouth then said, "I know that you were one of the airport's youngest pilots and one of the best J-3 Cub pilots on the field. You held the world's solo record when you were only sixteen, and you soloed ten different types of planes in one day. Right?" He grinned, chomping on a plug of tobacco.

"Right," I answered, squirming slightly.

He gave another chew then said, "They tell me you can fly helicopters and airplanes. You can repair or rebuild anything that flies. You even reconstructed a wrecked helicopter then went out and flew it." He looked at me thoughtfully for a second. "You live down the road in Fillmore and you're married to a lady named Judy. And you have two little girls."

I nodded. "Tami and Erica."

"And I know about your heart attack."

"It wasn't too serious," I said.

"I'm going to be honest with you, Grady. I won't ask you to do anything I wouldn't do, so how about it?" He held out his hand and I took it. The date was June 1, 1979.

A few days later I met Steve's lady, Barbara Jo Minty. She had driven up with Steve for the day from Malibu, where they were living. She was beautiful, in her mid-twenties, with long, dark hair worn in a pony tail. I had heard that she was a top fashion model and one look told me why. At a slim, statuesque five-feet-nine she stood just a few inches shorter than Steve. Her red shorts and tight-fitting rainbow-striped tank top set off not only her figure but her glowing tan. From the start she was friendly in a natural, unaffected way. Despite the difference in their ages—Steve was forty-nine—they made quite a pair.

The daily drive from Malibu to Santa Paula and back again set Steve thinking. He truly liked the old town of Santa Paula with its simple ways, its quaint atmosphere and slow-paced living. He could walk the streets and feel free, not imprisoned by watchful stares. "I've finally found what I've been looking for all these years," he told me. "and I'm really happy for once in my life. As a kid I lived near here at Meiner's Oaks. This country is as close to home as I can find. I want to die here." Within days Steve announced that he had decided to sell the Malibu house, adding, "I'm through with commuting. Until I can find a house in Santa Paula, Barbara and I will live in the hangar."

The northeast corner of the hangar was set aside for living quarters. Steve brought in a new box spring and mattress and placed them on the floor against the far wall. He added a dining table and some chairs. A makeshift rod served as a clothes closet. Nearby sat a portable television.

Soon the hangar took on the look of a museum. Steve was an avid collector and Barbara shared his enthusiasm. He had spent years gathering antique toys: cast iron cars, soldiers and tanks and ships, Buck Rogers guns, Kewpie dolls. He had old automotive display signs, rare neon signs, framed historic photos by the hundreds. There were old-fashioned cash registers and slot machines, bicycles and airplane propellers made of wood from another age, vintage gasoline pumps and jukeboxes with flashing colors. And of no less value was his incredible inventory of 140 classic motorcycles that included a 1914 Cyclone racer and a 1941 Indian. A favorite of his was a 1946 Chopper Indian which he was sure offered him some anonymity because it was so ratty. Among the others, all of which were kept in running condition, were those whose names were legend: Pierce Arrow, Crouch, Iver Johnson, Ace, Excelsior, Ner-A-Car, Cleveland, Pope, New Imperial, and Harley.

Some of the collection had been housed in Malibu, some in Beverly Hills (he kept a suite at one of the hotels where he stayed while working on film commitments), the rest in storage. Steve brought all of his collection to the hangar to take its place beside his two planes. Surrounded by this awesome display, he felt completely comfortable. He was in no hurry to find more suitable quarters, but the search was begun.

He decided he wanted to live in the country, away from the streets of town. One place that caught his attention early on was the Converse Ranch, a two-million-dollar spread that included a large old house and approximately twelve hundred acres. But the home imparted bad vibrations for both Steve and Barbara and they came away truly believing the place was haunted. Even later, reporting his feelings, Steve's eyes grew wide and he looked uncomfortable.

A short time later he heard about another ranch, this one tucked between two hills and only three miles from the airport. It was smaller than the Converse property, only fifteen acres, but to Steve the four-bedroom house seemed ideal. Admittedly, it needed some restoration, so before making a final decision he called his good friend, a carpenter, John Daly. John had worked closely with Steve in building the Malibu house.

John Daly remembers: "Steve told me he had finally found that little ranch house he had always wanted and asked if I thought it was restorable and worth the investment, having been built in 1896. On the backside of Santa Paula and typically Victorian in its architectural style, I based my value judgment more on my knowledge of McQueen and his personality than on the real estate itself. This house had Steve summed up to a tee, and though I knew it wouldn't be easy or cheap to do, the decision made itself."

On July 8 Steve signed the necessary papers and the ranch was his. During construction, however, he and Barbara decided to remain at the hangar.

John started to work almost immediately with one goal in mind: to recapture the original turn-of-the-century spirit of the house. As the days passed the project became even more of a challenge. Steve's list of changes went on and on.

Out went the near-new carpeting, installed throughout by the previous owner to impart a modern touch. What remained were the original hardwood floors to be sanded to their natural finish.

Next came a wall separating the two small bedrooms. Down it went to create new space for the master bedroom. A walk-in closet was on the drawing board, as was a spacious porch leading through new French doors from the master suite. Intricate Victorian pin rails (a series of tiny spindles) had to be duplicated to match those of the existing front porch.

For the living room, a raised fireplace of old brick,

flanked by an antique carved oak facing, mantel and book-shelves had to be designed. Steve discarded the existing mirror above the old mantel in favor of one with beveled edges, more authentic to the period.

Steve wanted crown moldings added around the four-teen-foot ceilings throughout. He found leaded stained glass windows for transom openings above doorways and for the bathrooms where old-fashioned toilets, complete with high wall-mounted tanks and chain pulls had been specified along with antique marble wash basins and brass fittings.

Steve and Barbara bought period ceiling fans for the dining room and master bedroom as well as Victorian multi-globe chandeliers. There were filigree light fixtures for the walls.

For the kitchen they found old-style appliances to replace the new. Even the counter tops had to be resur-faced with tiles from another period.

The master bathroom featured one of the few conces-sions to modern times: a spacious new shower, fully tiled in shades of blue.

As the work on the house progressed, Steve contin-ued his flight training. Under the guidance of Sammy and Pete Mason, he prepared for his private pilot license. He had taken the written examination and passed, but that was only half of it. He still had to pass the tough flight test, given by the Federal Aviation Agency.

There was some concern about his hearing, impaired by damage to his left eardrum in a diving accident many years earlier, although Steve never made much of it. His eyes weren't that good, either, particularly for close-up work, but he refused to have them examined. Instead he bought cheap plastic-rimmed bifocals from the dime store. He had boxes of them. He kept glasses everywhere, stuffed in shirt pockets and jackets, always within reach.

On July 20, 1979, Steve was elated to receive his radio communications license. Seven days later, after completing 133 hours of flying time, he took his flight test. It went smoothly, without a hitch, and Steve was granted a private pilot license. After that it was difficult keeping him on the ground.

On many of those warm summer mornings in 1979, Steve was in the air shortly after sunrise. "He got up with the chickens," Barbara would say with a smile, "and flew away."

Steve's flight would often take him eastward some forty-five air miles to Aqua Dulce, a near-abandoned strip situated in an old mining region high in the mountains. Sometimes he'd fly to nearby Indian Dunes where he met with old friends and new. The foothills adjacent to the runway at Indian Dunes often teemed with bikers racing the hilly course. It was an area Steve knew well from his dirt bike days.

Barbara had interests of her own. She kept an active eye on the daily progress of the ranch house restoration and decorating. There were curtains to buy, wallpaper to select, color schemes to mull over. Outside, gardens needed planning and enclosures had to be considered: pens and coops and corrals, soon to be filled with rabbits, goats, geese, chickens, and horses. And, of course, there'd be dogs and cats. Dressed for hands-and-knees work, Barbara was beautiful as she wandered about the cultivated land, or drove to the local feed store to check available supplies. Steve appreciated her efforts and encouraged them. One day she returned with eight laying hens. They both thrilled at the new life they were creating.

In mid-August Steve asked me to pick up a 1946 army Jeep he had bought from Universal Studios. I was also to bring back the new clothes he'd ordered from a sporting goods store in Beverly Hills. On the way home, with the Jeep in tow, a highway patrol officer stopped me for driving too slowly in the freeway fast lane. He was a no-nonsense guy at first, but once he saw Steve's name on the car registration, and I told him I worked for Steve, his attitude softened. "We used to go after Steve a lot for speeding," he grinned, "but half the time we couldn't catch up with him. He'd outrun us." He handed back the slips of paper without writing a ticket. "Tell Steve his friends on the force said hello." Then he drove off.

Not many days later, Steve's producer, Mort Engleberg, arrived in Santa Paula to discuss plans for a new film, *The Hunter*. Few scripts excited Steve, but this, the true story of Ralph "Papa" Thorson, king of the bounty hunters, was one he believed in. Another consideration may have been that Steve hadn't been before a camera for over six months, not since completing *Tom Horn* just before he'd come to Santa Paula.

The Hunter was to be filmed in Chicago over a five-week period. With the Santa Paula ranch in chaos from remodeling it seemed a perfect time for Steve and Barbara to be gone. But Steve was concerned. He feared leaving the ranch and hangar unattended, stocked with his valuables. "It's a lifetime of sentiment," he told me. "It's everything I own."

Someone had to keep a watchful eye, especially with workmen coming and going. But five weeks! It wasn't that long a time, I told myself. There was plenty to keep me busy; the days would pass quickly. I volunteered to stay.

"No," Steve said, his eyes crinkling. "I don't want to take you away from your family."

I told him not to worry about it. Judy would understand.

He turned away, thoughtful. Then, "Well, only if it's all right with her."

That evening I explained the situation to Judy. The thought of a separation, however brief, was at first discomforting to her so I dropped the subject. A short time later she said, "If the girls were younger we'd come and stay with you. But they're in school so that's out." She smiled compassionately. "It's important to Steve. He's counting on you—you can't let him down." At the time, neither of us realized that we would be facing many similar separations over the coming months.

When I made the offer to Steve I didn't know where I'd be living. The ranch house was too torn up. Then I remembered the mobile home. Along with the property came a 1978 Canyon Crest model. It was seventy feet long, twelve feet wide and stood unoccupied on the east side of the driveway leading up to the house. I couldn't imagine how ideal it would be until I got inside.

The interior was like new, completely furnished and paneled. There were two bedrooms and two baths, one featuring a sunken Turkish tub and a shower. The kitchen was fully equipped with built-ins, including a garbage disposal. There was even a telephone. I wouldn't be completely cut off from Judy and the kids, after all. And less than a half-mile away, Clete Roberts kept his trailer. I knew I could count on seeing a friendly face when Clete came to Santa Paula on weekends.

Steve called every morning from Chicago, always at an ungodly hour. He thought nothing of phoning at 6:00 A.M. before leaving for the day's shooting—6:00 A.M. Chicago time, 4:00 A.M. in California! Never did he call to chat idly. He wanted questions answered and jobs done. How was the house coming along? Had the painters started? How were his planes faring without him? He wanted fields plowed, corrals built, the chicken coops enlarged. Would I check out security systems for both the house and the hangar? He decided it was time to start planting around the front property line. He particularly liked *myoporum* (a dense, evergreen shrub with shiny dark green leaves). "We want lots of them," he said, "planted close together. And they have to be specimen size, not young plants." He wanted his privacy without having to wait for it.

As the weeks passed, Steve's interest never flagged but he was sounding tired. Some days were rough, he admitted, more strenuous than he had anticipated. It was all he could do to keep up with the fast-paced action and prepare himself for the next day's shooting.

The Hunter went several weeks over schedule, delaying Steve and Barbara's return to Santa Paula until mid-October. Once home, however, Steve's commitment to the film continued. Additional footage still had to be shot, both at Paramount Studios in Los Angeles and at other Southern California locations. But, for Steve, it really didn't matter since the ranch house wasn't quite ready to occupy. He and Barbara decided to stay in the city during the work week and return on weekends to their makeshift quarters in the hangar.

They seemed happy to be back in Santa Paula, if only for short periods. There was so much new to see and do, weeks of progress to check out and discover.

One afternoon Steve wandered through the empty house where he found John Daly busy on some last-minute touch-up work. Steve decided it was time for John to take a break and the two men walked outside onto the newly completed porch. For a while they sat silently, looking out at the lemon trees and nearby hillsides, breathing the scent of citrus. At last Steve said, "I can't tell you how many times I've sworn I'd take off to a mountain cabin somewhere and do nothing but think." He grinned. "Well, I'm here."

Steve was silent again for several moments. Then, in a serious voice he said, "John, I've got this cough that's really bugging me. Funny, it only comes on at night."

John didn't read much into the remark. He replied, simply, "Why not get it checked out? If it's anything serious you'll have a chance to clear it up. If it's nothing you won't have to worry anymore."

Steve's eyes crinkled. "I hate going to doctors," he said. Then he fell silent again.

John didn't comment further. Although he was always willing to offer Steve an opinion, he never told him what to do. "And I don't know of anyone who ever did," he said later.

Chapter Two

October drew slowly to a close. The days grew noticeably shorter and the nights longer, almost endless. The fact that Steve and Barbara were within a few hours' drive working in Los Angeles (or "town," as Steve put it) meant little. Life at the ranch, from sunset to dawn, was a lonely, often eerie existence.

The windows of the mobile home that had been my shelter for nearly two months directly overlooked the dark and empty ranch house. Surrounded by the blackness of night, with moonlight accentuating the sharp lines and gingerbread trim, the view for me became a scene from Hitchcock's *Psycho*. Aside from Clete Roberts' trailer, which stood lifeless from Monday through Friday, only one other house was within walking distance. But it too was deserted.

Through the stillness came the endless chirp of crickets and, from a small swamp at the base of the cliffs, the croaking of a thousand frogs; in the distance the monotonous creaking-thumping of oil pumps, drawing black gold from beneath the ground.

One evening, as I sat working by the light of the tack room, a shadow caught my attention. It was in the shape of a man. He was standing at a window, inside one of the bedrooms of the house.

I hurried to the mobile home for my pistol and a flashlight, then cautiously approached the dark building. Gun in hand I moved from room to room, shining the light in all directions. I found nothing.

When Steve and Barbara returned from town late that Friday afternoon I hesitated to mention the incident. Steve, after all, had been visibly upset over less when he'd visited the Converse Ranch. Intuitively, I bypassed him and told Barbara, knowing she would understand, especially if I made light of it.

No sooner were the words out than Barbara turned to Steve and said, "Hey, honey, guess what Grady saw the other night. A ghost!"

Steve's eyes grew wide. "That's all I need," he said, "a haunted house! Why don't you tell me some good news?" He was silent for a moment, then, "Tell me exactly what you saw, Grady."

I repeated the story, trying to be even less serious than before. I even made a point of stressing my overactive imagination.

Steve nodded several times then changed the subject. He wanted me to join him and Barbara for dinner.

The three of us climbed into Steve's Chevy pickup and drove to the Old Gang Coffee Shop, his favorite place to eat in downtown Santa Paula. The Old Gang was clean but small and far from fancy. But it was a popular gathering spot for townspeople and had been since its old Mu Pu Indian Grill days.

There were two things Steve especially liked about the place: halibut steak, prepared just as he ordered, *burned,* and the all-female staff. Without question, Steve believed that women not only cooked but served better than men. His feelings went far deeper than that, however. His old-fashioned perspective on life strongly influenced his values. In Steve's world, men gave orders and women obeyed.

Midway through dinner Steve began acting strangely. He became withdrawn, dropping out of the conversation to stare into space. Then, quite suddenly, he put his fork aside and in a serious way said, "Grady, tell me one more time what you saw the other night."

I turned, half-smiling, to Barbara. She too appeared concerned, not about the incident but Steve's reaction to it. "It was nothing, Steve," I replied. "A reflection or something, that's all."

He didn't press on. For a time I thought the matter had been forgotten.

I met Steve at the hangar early the following morning. He sat on a stool at his workbench, changing tires on an antique toy car (he kept an entire drawer filled with tiny white rubber replacements). In his mouth he had a wad of chewing tobacco; from time to time he took aim at the spit can near his feet. Barbara was still asleep in the far corner bed.

Steve didn't hear me come in. It wasn't until I was standing at his side that he noticed me. He turned, peering over the tops of his bifocals and said, smiling, "'Morning, Grady."

He continued to work while I crossed the hangar to the kitchenette and poured a cup of coffee. When I returned he said, without looking up, "I've been thinking . . . "

Steve talked of his plan to construct a large building to store his impressive collection of antique cars: the 1939 Packard, the 1950 Hudson Wasp, the 1957 Allard, the Jaguar XKSS, and the others (there were more than forty automobiles in all). The new building would be located to the east of the house, on land where the mobile home now stood. He was anxious to get started on it.

"What about the mobile home?" I asked. Over the weeks I'd grown rather fond of the place.

"It's yours if you can find a place in Santa Paula to park it," he answered, still engrossed in his work. "Otherwise, I'll sell it."

"Then you're moving into the house soon?"

He put his glasses aside and swiveled around on the stool. "Not for a while. I still have a few weeks left on the picture."

Something was strange, I told myself. I looked him straight in the eyes. He returned the stare, trying to keep a straight face. He couldn't.

"And what did you have in mind for me?" I asked.

"Well," he grinned boyishly, "I thought you'd like to get out of the mobile home for a while. You'd have a lot more room in the house and you'd be able to check out the—"

"Ghosts?"

"That's not what I had in mind, but since you brought it up."

"Forget it. I'm just as big a chicken as you are."

"It's the only way, Grady."

I thought of stalling him. The mobile home was huge; a monster, a great white elephant. It would take two spaces at least in a trailer park and all the ones around Santa Paula had waiting lists. But I'd have Judy call anyway—that would take some time. Finding a buyer wouldn't be easy either.

"And don't go puttin' this off," he added. "I want to get rid of that thing by next weekend."

"I could make a bed in the tack room," I said. "Any place, but not in the house."

"You can't stay out there. You'll freeze your rear end off."

I reminded him of his words when he hired me. "Didn't you say you wouldn't ask me to do anything you wouldn't do?"

He swiveled back to the workbench and put on his glasses. "Oh, yeah," he said mischievously, "how about that?"

I had to laugh. Here we were, two grown men acting like kids spooked by the boogeyman. There was no reason to be afraid; I'd proved that to myself. Steve, on the other hand, had to take my word for it. In all fairness to him, never again did he ask me to do anything he wouldn't do.

I immediately set out to find a buyer for the mobile home. It wasn't as difficult as I anticipated. Tony Pollack, owner of the local golf course, made a quick, generous offer.

When I returned to the hangar with the news around noon on Sunday, Steve was polishing the Pitcairn Mailwing. Actually, he was caressing the plane. He had a look in his eyes. It was easy to read what was on his mind. He had ridden in the plane with Sammy Mason at the single controls. Sammy had even soloed the plane long enough to learn its characteristics and provide Steve with a verbal checkout. Still, after all these months, Steve had not taken it up. The Pitcairn continued to sit idly in the hangar.

The Pitcairn was a large biplane with a big engine that obscured forward visibility, making takeoffs and landings a bit tricky. The plane represented a challenge to Steve, and it ate at him. That Sunday, as he worked his polishing cloth across the Pitcairn's shiny forest green surface, he had only one thought in mind.

"Do you think I can fly it?" he asked suddenly.

Steve had become a good pilot in a relatively short time. Without hesitating, I told him the words he wanted to hear.

"I'll tell you what," he said, a slight uneasiness in his voice, "I won't fly it now. I'll just taxi up and down the runway to practice getting the feel of it." A moment later we were pushing the plane out of the hangar.

Steve climbed into the cockpit and put on his helmet and goggles, then buckled his shoulder harness and safety belt. "Turn the prop through a couple of times, Grady, while I prime the engine."

I walked to the front of the plane and thrust the propeller blade downward.

"That's good," he hollered. "Clear prop!"

As I moved aside, the engine fired. After a brief warm-up Steve slowly maneuvered the plane to the runway. Then he made several runs back and forth.

At times he would get up enough speed to raise the tail off the ground. He handled the rudder very well, keeping the plane straight down the runway. Down and back he came; I never took my eyes from him.

Soon Steve was taxiing back to the hangar, shutting the engine down. He remained seated, a glazed look in his eyes. "Boy, I don't know," he sighed.

Before I could say anything, Barbara drove up in her old 1953 pickup truck, nicknamed Cline. Steve jumped from the plane to give her a welcoming hug. They talked for a moment then Steve asked me to join them for lunch.

During the drive to the airport cafe, through lunch and our return to the hangar the conversation never varied. The Pitcairn was the sole subject. Steve had been bitten by the bug; now that he'd been at the controls he wanted more. But he also realized that taxiing the plane up and down the runway required only a fraction of the skills necessary for flying. He was stubborn enough to want to be airborne but smart enough not to exceed his capabilities. The Pitcairn was now his master. He would not be happy until he was in charge.

"You can do it, Steve," I pushed. "I watched you this morning. You can handle the plane."

"I don't know, Grady. It's pretty squirrelly on the ground."

"Get in it. Fly it!"

He shook his head. "I'll have to think about it for a while," he said, starting for his workbench. But he was back in a minute saying, "I'm awfully tempted."

I didn't let up. "It's now or never, Steve."

He took a deep breath, then slowly exhaled, "Okay, Grady, this is it!"

By the time Steve had warmed the engine a few friends and spectators had gathered outside the hangar. Steve checked the runway to see if the final approach was clear. Finding it open he taxied out and shoved the throttle in. Seconds later he was airborne.

Barbara and I stood together as the Pitcairn left the ground. She too shared Steve's enthusiasm for flying and would soon begin taking lessons on her own. "He's on his way," I said.

Barbara nodded, "Now all he has to do is land it." She was smiling but there was a note of apprehension in her voice.

Steve circled the airport once then maneuvered into the approach pattern for landing. Slowly he eased the plane down, careful to clear the fence at the base of the runway. He came in on two wheels, straight and level, a perfect landing.

A round of applause greeted Steve as he pulled off the

runway and taxied back to the hangar. He had a big grin on his face that seemed to say, *I did it!*

I hurried to congratulate him as he jumped from the plane. We shook hands and he said, "You had more faith in me than I did, pal."

"How did you feel?"

He grinned. "Scared to death. If it hadn't been for you I'd never left the ground. But I'm glad I did."

"I knew you could do it, Steve. I never had any doubts."

"Yeah?"

"Most people would have fooled around taxiing up and down the runway. You got right into position and flew off."

"Well, I'll tell you," he said quietly, "with all those people standing around I figured I'd better go ahead and get it over with. I didn't want to disappoint anybody."

Later that afternoon Steve dragged his old desk chair outside the hangar where we sat, watching the sun set and drinking beer. Suddenly he got up and went inside. When he came back he was carrying a large book on the history of aviation, one from his personal collection. "I'd like you to have this," he said.

I opened the front cover. Inside he had written: "To Grady, Thanks for all your help—*pushing* me in the air. Steve McQueen, Santa Paula Airport '79."

On Monday, after Steve and Barbara left for Los Angeles, I began making preparations to have the mobile home moved to its new location at the golf course. There wasn't any rush really, as long as it was gone by their return on Friday afternoon. That suited me fine; I was in no hurry to set up housekeeping in the ranch house.

On Friday evening I moved my few belongings inside. The house was completely empty, not one piece of furniture had been brought in, so I had my pick of the rooms. I chose to stay in the living room. It was in the center of the house; the best vantage point, I figured, should anything happen.

My bed was made of blankets on the floor directly in front of the fireplace. I crawled in that evening with all the lights on, the burglar alarm set, and my pistol beside me. Sleep did not come easily.

The next morning I dragged myself to the hangar to report to Steve and Barbara. They took one look at me and burst into laughter. "Do I look that bad?" I asked.

Steve doubled up.

"You look fine, Grady," Barbara said. "It's something else." Then she started roaring again.

Steve finally calmed down enough to say, "I had an idea last night. I told Barb we ought to put sheets over our heads and go over to the ranch and scare Grady."

"Is that right?" I mumbled.

"But I was afraid you might shoot us," he went on, "so we decided not to come."

A wise decision, I emphasized.

The following Sunday, Steve invited a few friends to the hangar to help celebrate his soloing the Pitcairn. It was quite a gathering. From the airport came pilots Perry Schreffler, Art Rink, Bob Van Osdale, Doug Dullenkopf, Mike and Jeanette Dewey, Chuck and Annie Sisto; mechanics Wayne Munter, Lou Boyce and Mark Thoms, as well as Betty Hurt, head waitress at the airport cafe. From Santa Paula came Willard and Jennie Beckley and their daughter, Cynthia; Bruce and Patty Dickinson and his father, Don. From Los Angeles came director Cliff Coleman and actor Lee Majors. Lee had driven to Santa Paula earlier in the day to congratulate Steve on his flying fete, knowing nothing about the party. He agreed to stay long enough to join in a toast and some flight talk before heading home. Lee's television series, *The Six Million Dollar Man*, had featured a number of helicopter sequences.

Steve had hoped to keep the guest list down, but that was impossible. Visitors to the airport, attracted by the festivities, streamed inside, and before long Steve was running low on beer and ice. I made a quick trip into town to bolster the supplies.

Steve had once remarked that if he found himself in a room with more than five people he'd get up and leave. The hangar now teemed with ten times that many, and his discomfort was clearly showing. He cornered me to say, "Keep your eyes open, Grady. I don't want anyone lifting anything."

As the minutes passed Steve grew progressively edgy. Suddenly, and without warning, he shouted, "Sorry, folks, the party's over."

A few people started moving out through the large opening of the hangar, but not enough. Steve pushed a button and the automatic doors began closing. Only then did the remaining guests take him seriously, and they quickly departed out the side door. Later, with Barbara, Judy, and me, he joked, "There sure were a bunch of people here. There mustn't be anything to do in these parts but party."

By early November, Steve was fairly convinced that the ranch house was not ghost ridden. At least he felt it was safe enough to bring in a few pieces of furniture. A large circular oak table for the dining room and an antique sofa were the first to arrive. Next came some of Steve's prized possessions, which were to receive special placement. Included were deer heads, antlers, old photos (some of early motorcycles, others Western in theme) and rare movie posters, an antique gas pump, a 1940s jukebox, an Indian motorcycle, gum and candy machines, a saddle, and his guns and gun racks. When Barbara's books arrived they were placed on the shelves beside the new fireplace.

Though still basically unfurnished, the house was beginning to take on a warm, homey look. When Barbara confided that she had grown tired of living in the hangar—and complained, "There isn't room to put anything!"—I cornered Steve. "Come over to the house tonight," I said, "and have a look around. You'll like it."

He agreed to stop by.

It was chilly that evening. I had a fire blazing in the fireplace and lights glowed in every room. Steve wandered about, pleased to see so many familiar things at every turn.

Steve asked for a beer. When I returned from the kitchen he and Barbara were in the living room stretched out on the sofa, Steve with his feet resting on an old coffee table. He was looking at the deer head that hung from the wall above the mantel. "Boy, this is really nice," he said, taking a sip. Then he put his head back and closed his eyes.

"When are you and Barbara moving in?" I asked, subtly.

The Hunter was nearly completed, he said. All the photography had been shot, and only a few more weeks of "looping" remained to synchronize the sound track with the film.

"We won't have to go into town so often for that," Barbara said. "Maybe a couple of times more, that's all." She smiled.

We waited for a comment from Steve but it didn't come. He had dozed off.

The following day the three of us went to a nearby nursery. Barbara was anxious to buy indoor plants for the house. She and Steve also wanted to look at outdoor trees for the yard. They talked of doing the planting themselves, for sentimental reasons.

We took the van, which had two seats up front. I

drove, leaving the other for Steve and Barbara. They didn't seem to mind the crowded conditions. In fact, they thought it an ideal arrangement; he could hug her in his arms along the way. The open display of affection was understandable. Steve told me that he loved Barbara more than any lady in his life.

As we pulled up to the nursery I was cautioned, "Remember, don't let them add the movie star tax." It was a line I'd heard before. Steve was always fearful that people would try to take advantage of him. He felt they saw him coming and, knowing his reputation for making big bucks, would up the selling price.

By the time we left the nursery the van was stocked with green plants. Steve took one look at the potted jungle and, with an expression of submission, sighed, "With all this stuff we're going to *have* to make the move."

Barbara kept the pressure on. Hardly a day passed without a shipment arriving for the house. A huge antique stove was delivered, and an old General Electric refrigerator with double doors and a tower of coils. There were chairs and lamps and tables—and shiny brass spittoons, one for each room.

Two brass beds were brought in, one king size for the master bedroom and a double bed for the second bedroom (the third was turned into a storeroom). "That'll be Grady's room," Steve joked. But he was half-serious. He knew that once I returned to my family there would still be nights I'd be working late. He would insist that I stay rather than drive back to the apartment in Fillmore.

The steady stream of incoming furnishings did not surprise me. Barbara was simply ticking off the days, preparing for that long-awaited moment when Steve would finally say, "Let's go." What did surprise me was the sight of his clothes, armful upon armful being brought in and carefully arranged on his side of the new walk-in wardrobe closet.

There were plaid flannel shirts in all colors, leather vests and jackets, jeans, T-shirts, slacks, sport coats and suits with expensive labels. There were boxes full of shoes—work shoes, house shoes, tennis shoes, dress shoes, sandals and boots; socks by the gross; caps and hats, including the Western hat he wore in *Tom Horn*.

By mid-November Steve announced that all post-production work on *The Hunter* was completed. The trips to Los Angeles were over. Steve and Barbara were moving out of the hangar, and I could at last rejoin Judy and the children. As I left, I couldn't resist one parting shot, "Don't let the ghost get you."

"Oh, go home, Grady!" Steve teased.

I practically flew the fifteen miles to the apartment. For the first time since early September I'd be spending the night under the same roof with Judy, Erica and Tami.

With Steve and Barbara's move to the house came a new routine. I'd arrive in the mornings to find Barbara in the kitchen fixing breakfast. She'd pour a cup of her wondrous coffee, made from freshly ground beans as Steve liked it, and we'd chat. Then Steve would appear, usually in his heavy brown robe and fur-lined leather slippers. He'd stand in the bedroom doorway, his hair tousled, and invite me inside while he dressed. "We have some things to discuss," he'd say. At first I hesitated, but he'd wave me in. "You're part of the family now, so that's enough of that subject."

In the early mornings we'd talk about the plans for the coming day. In the late afternoons, by the warmth of the smudge pot just outside the tack room, we'd review our accomplishments. It was at those times, with his cap pushed back, a beer in his hand and his cheek puffed out with chewing tobacco, Steve seemed most relaxed.

One afternoon, as the sun disappeared behind the hills and the sky grew slowly darker, Steve said, "I'd like you and your family to go with Barb and me to church on Sunday." The remark caught me off guard, especially when he added, "I'd like you to learn more about God. It'll make a difference in your life."

I wasn't a regular churchgoer and Steve knew it. But then he hadn't been either until the past spring when he began attending Ventura Missionary Church. Steve hadn't talked much about religion, although he did mention earlier that he had received some training in childhood in his mother's Catholic faith, which had failed to "stick" with him. "For years," he had said, "my God and religion were the green grass, the sky, and motorcycles. I thought everything else was a lot of hocus-pocus. But I met some pretty fine people from the church, guys that were pretty tough onions."

It was Sammy Mason who rekindled Steve's interest in religion. Years earlier Sammy had introduced me to the church, promising flying lessons if I would attend. Steve was attracted in a similar way during the long hours he and Sammy spent together as part of Steve's flight training.

Sammy, a devout Christian, has described himself as "grumpy, hard to get along with, and a recluse," characteristics that had, at times, been identified with Steve. Their first contact was far from smooth. Each held stubbornly to his own thinking; Steve would only have Sammy as his teacher, but Sammy had no time for Steve. Once they met, things were different—perhaps because, on the surface, they were so similar. As Sammy has stated, "I doubt that any friendship developed as quickly, or had more depth, than ours. We talked intimately about our feelings about life and our purpose for being here."

Religion played a major role in drawing the two men closer together. Sammy Mason remembers: "When Steve learned I was a Christian he asked if he could attend church with me. In a short time he learned to love the God who had sacrificed His Son out of love for mankind.

"From that moment on I saw a dramatic change in Steve. I had always felt that he possessed a depth of character, but when Christ infiltrated his life and brought it in tune with God's will, the full beauty of the man began to blossom. Oh, he still had problems with his quick temper and with areas of his life that had been poorly cultivated for many years, but I doubt that I have ever seen a man flourish with more spiritual reality in such a short time."

John Daly, too, could see the change in Steve. He first noticed it that day in late June when he rode out to the ranch with Steve to offer his opinion on the house. John, who hadn't seen Steve in nearly two years, said, "Steve began to relate to me how he'd gotten very serious about giving his heart to Jesus and how, through the influence of Sammy Mason, he'd even started going to church on Sundays, 'a good solid church,' as he put it, and that 'the Lord was rearranging his life to be more upright.' Few people could understand the magnitude of this miracle because so very few people really knew of the bizarre background this man had come from.

"I thought back on how Steve had once told me about sincerely recognizing his need for God—how he looked at me and said, 'I've had so many close calls with death that sometimes I wonder why I'm still alive. It's like someone has been watching over me, taking care of me so many, many times.' I think I had more faith that my saw and hammer would have gotten converted before Steve, but I was hearing it from the horse's mouth. I was blown away."

The Sunday following Steve's invitation, Judy, the girls, and I joined Steve and Barbara for church. We drove separately, Steve leading the way in his 1950 Hudson Wasp while my family and I followed in the pickup truck. For some reason, Steve had decided to take Foothill Road into Ventura rather than the freeway. We'd gotten off to a late start and Steve was determined to make the eight o'clock service. Over the narrow, winding road we raced, hitting the curves at breakneck speed. It was like a scene from *Bullitt.*

Steve preferred sitting in the balcony, away from the crowd of worshipers. As his pastor Leonard DeWitt remarked, "He wasn't there to be seen of men but to commune with God." Nor was he one to linger following the services. Steve was usually the first to depart.

Pastor DeWitt recalled a meeting with Steve just prior to the start of filming on *The Hunter:* "One Sunday morning after Steve and Barbara had been attending church for a few months, he came to me and wanted to know if we could get together for lunch. We set up a time and I met him at the Santa Paula Airport restaurant. For over two hours all I did was answer his questions about the Christian life. When it appeared he had no more to ask I said, 'Steve, I have just one question for you.' With a big smile he said, 'You want to know if I have become a born-again Christian.' I replied, 'That's right. To me that is the most important question.' Still smiling, but very serious, he responded, 'Yes, I have asked Jesus Christ to take over my life.'"

It was about this time that Steve heard Kris Kristofferson's recording of *Why Me, Lord?* and it immediately became one of his favorites; he identified with it, relating the moving lyrics to his new life in the most positive way. Steve was deeply thankful for all the good that had come to him during the past year.

Success as Steve knew it had not necessarily brought contentment. And while on the surface he seemed to be one of the chosen few, something was missing—that glow or inner peace that made Sammy Mason and John Daly "different." But since coming to Santa Paula, new horizons opened to him. God had entered Steve's life; he had accepted the gospel. Now, with the ongoing fulfillment of his spiritual hunger, Steve felt as if the Lord had truly singled him out. Rarely a day passed that he didn't count his blessings. Even later, during the darkest of times, Steve heard only good in the Kristofferson recording. He never once asked "Why me, Lord?" in a negative way.

In the months that followed, my family and I would accompany Steve and Barbara many times. It had always been difficult to get me in church, but Steve, with his low-key, persuasive ways and deep beliefs, succeeded. There were Sundays, however, when I felt I should stay behind. "I have things to take care of," I'd tell him, or "I'd better watch over the ranch today." He'd never push. He'd simply say, "Okay, pal." But then he'd phone Judy and ask her and the children to go.

Most people who had known Steve for years, like John Daly, noticed the changes in his behavior. He had mellowed, they said, become more passive and even-tempered. But there were times when I saw the Steve of old. One morning I arrived at the ranch to find him in a fitful mood. Unlike Barbara, Steve was a sound sleeper. She complained of the night sounds—the crickets and frogs and, most especially, the creaking of the oil pumps down the road—that disrupted the normal stillness. Steve never heard them. But early that morning, around two o'clock, the burglar alarm suddenly went off. The system was quite complicated, involving a keyboard on which a combination of numbers was set. When the alarm sounded, sending its piercing scream into the night, Steve bolted upright in bed. He ran to the keyboard to shut it off but no matter which buttons he pushed the sound continued. In a fit of anger he ripped all the wires from the alarm's main power box. He was still fuming when he reported the incident to the alarm company, demanding that the entire system be removed from his house.

By the time a company representative arrived that afternoon Steve had calmed down somewhat, and he agreed to let the system remain. But it took the repairmen a week to right the damage he had done.

Not many days later, Steve, Barbara, and I were out by the corrals when Steve noticed one of the horses—Barbara had brought in seven from her ranch in Idaho—bump against a railing, causing the post to give considerably. We went to investigate. Not only was that post loose, so were most of the others. Norman, one of Steve's carpenters happened to be standing by. "Sometimes the fence companies take shortcuts," Norman said. "They dig the hole as specified but only put a small ring of cement at the top and bottom to save on costs."

Steve had Norman dig around one of the posts. Norman was right; the hole was not completely filled with cement, only a small ring at the top. Steve was furious. He was on the phone in minutes demanding to speak with the president of the company.

An executive was at the ranch in no time, following Steve from post to post, noting them wobble. "This isn't right, partner," Steve said, his eyes narrowed. "I made a deal with you to put these corrals in and look what you give me!"

The executive was not intimidated. Calmly, he replied, "But, Mr. McQueen, it's your soil. It's loose."

"Don't give me that!" Steve roared. "There just ain't enough cement around these poles."

The man smiled. "We just recently completed a job in Las Vegas for Wayne Newton, one very similar to yours, and he hasn't complained."

Steve looked ready to punch the guy. "I'm not Wayne Newton," he said through firmly clenched teeth, "and I don't like the way you did this job. Either you make it right or I call my attorney and we settle it that way. And that's my last word on the matter."

The man didn't take a moment to weigh his choices. He would send a crew out in the morning to correct the work. As he drove off in his shiny new car, Steve turned and said, "I don't like to be rude but sometimes I have to be just to keep people off my back." He had another way of putting it. As he told the cabinetmaker who had tried to take advantage of him on a job at the hangar: "I don't mind getting screwed, but I don't like getting screwed royally."

Steve kept a close eye on the repair work around the corrals. One afternoon Barbara and I joined him in the inspection. When we were done we followed the road up the hill that led to a plateau overlooking the ranch. Midway there Steve began slowing down, finally having to stop to catch his breath. We rested awhile until he felt better, then continued on. As we neared the plateau, he stopped again. "Aren't you winded, Grady?" he asked, panting.

I answered, "No, just a little tired, that's all."

His chest was heaving as he strained for air. "Well, maybe it's because I have a bad lung," he mumbled.

He had mentioned a damaged lung before, but only in passing. It had collapsed, the result of a battery explosion in an armored vehicle when he was in the service years before. As he explained, "The thing practically blew up in my face."

Barbara and I waited until Steve was breathing normally again. Then we turned about and made our way back down the hill.

The next morning Steve seemed in good spirits. He felt fine, he said, and was anxious to get started with the day's activities. The workmen were arriving to begin construction on the big storehouse for his antique cars; the idea of a hothouse, where he and Barbara could grow their own vegetables, intrigued him and a site had to be selected; his newly purchased Kubota tractor was waiting to be mastered—and how better to learn than by grading the dirt in the corrals?

Steve approached every task, every goal with patience and determination. He had credited his great success as an actor to "time, study, and lots of preparation," but that same philosophy applied to all aspects of his life. He never had the benefit of extended schooling. He learned by doing; hour upon hour, day after day until he was satisfied with the results of his efforts. Above all, he was not one to quit. None of us knew then that this unrelenting tenacity would soon be tested to the fullest.

Later that afternoon we drove to the airport for our end-of-day relaxation. Steve liked to roll his old desk chair out in front of the hangar doors and, leaning back with beer in hand, watch the planes take off and land. He had finished one can and was starting another when he remarked, "This beer tastes awful." He made a face then added, jokingly, "They told me if I started going to church I'd lose my taste for it. I guess they were right." He smiled as he stared off in the distance. A moment later he excused himself, saying, "I'm going to lie down for a while."

That evening at home Judy suggested inviting Steve and Barbara to our apartment for Thanksgiving dinner, three days away. Judy and Barbara were fast becoming friends. They shopped together and recently had selected several pieces of white wicker furniture for Steve's new porch. Sometimes they met for lunch. Steve felt comfortable around Tami and Erica. He loved children.

The next morning I approached Barbara. "I'm sorry," she said, regretfully, "Steve isn't feeling very well. His chest and back are bothering him." I kept the invitation open hoping that by Thursday he'd be better. He wasn't. He continued working around the ranch but without his usual zest and energy; he appeared simply to be going through the motions. His discomfort was obvious, and he expressed concern over his right lung, his good lung.

On Saturday, Steve visited neighbor Clete Roberts, driving his Chevy pickup over the small rise to Clete's trailer. Clete was somewhat surprised when Steve refused his offer of a beer. "I only drink cheap stuff," Steve alibied, and Clete stocked a German brand. Then Steve confessed that he had been feeling poorly of late. He told Clete of his accident while in the service—the exploding battery which, he said, had left him not only with a badly damaged lung but a number of broken bones. For proof, he had Clete feel the fractures still evident in his chest and back and rib cage. "I suppose I should get myself fixed up," Steve said, "but it would take six months for me to recover. To hell with that!"

Within a few days Steve was back at the airport, flying again. He insisted he felt better, well enough at least to visit friends at his old haunts, Aqua Dulce and Indian Dunes. Barbara too was adding to her flight time. She had taken her training in a Decathlon and now had a plane of her own, a mint condition Piper Cub J-3 which Steve had purchased for her.

The soreness in Steve's chest continued to bother him. Some days were better than others, he'd admit, but the problem had lingered too long, this time over three weeks, without noticeable relief. There was no cause for alarm, he felt certain, but why let it persist? A shot or prescription may be all that was needed to clear things up and set his mind at ease. On December 10, despite earlier vows, he decided to call one of the doctors at Santa Paula Hospital. Chest x-rays were taken that day.

Steve didn't have long to wait for the results. Within a few hours the hospital was on the phone reporting that the x-rays revealed a spot on his right lung. Steve wasted no time; I was immediately sent to retrieve the x-rays, and deliver them to his personal doctor at Cedars-Sinai Medical Center in Los Angeles for closer study.

On my return I found Steve sitting out by the tack room. He had been thinking, and not about himself. "I want you to have a complete physical," he told me. "The works, everything. Make an appointment and I'll pay for it."

I looked at him blankly. What was he talking about?

"I want to make sure that you're all right," he said. "And no more long hours. There's no reason to work so hard around here. We have plenty of time to get things done."

It would have been pointless to argue. Nor did I try to change the subject. Anything to keep his mind off his own worries. Absentmindedly, I lit a cigarette.

"And another thing," he went on, "no more cigarettes. Every time I see you smoking I'm going to get after you— and I'm going to keep doing it until you quit."

I let the cigarette fall to the ground, pulverizing it with the heel of my boot. If Steve could stop—and he confessed to being up to three packs a day at one time—so could I. At least around him.

Several days later, Steve's doctor phoned. There was no doubt; the x-rays clearly revealed a spot on his right lung. Steve would have to be admitted to the hospital for further tests.

Barbara would accompany Steve to Los Angeles and remain with him throughout his stay in the hospital. They had no idea how long that would be, but as Steve remarked as they walked to the car, "I feel pretty optimistic about it."

Chapter Three

Steve was admitted to Cedars-Sinai Medical Center on Monday, December 17, 1979, under the assumed name of Don Schoonover. He wanted to keep his identity a secret, not because of his career. He'd had too little time to think about that. The doctors' reports had been too shocking and had come without warning. At this point, Steve simply wanted his privacy; he treasured that. But a change of name wasn't precaution enough. Word that Steve McQueen was a patient soon spread throughout the hospital.

The following day, Barbara phoned the ranch. She spoke so softly I hardly recognized her voice. The results of Steve's new tests and x-rays were in, she said, adding, "It's not the best news, I'm afraid." Taking a deep breath, she went on. "They're planning to operate . . . exploratory surgery. They want to biopsy some of Steve's lung tissue."

Her words frightened me but I tried not to let on. "When?" I asked.

"Saturday morning."

"I'm driving down, Barb. I want to be with you and Steve."

Barbara was silent several seconds. Then, almost in a whisper, she said, "Thanks, Grady. I was hoping you'd say that."

I phoned Judy immediately.

"Do you think it would be all right if I called Steve?" she wondered. "I want him to know that our prayers are with him."

"I'm sure he'd like that," I answered.

She told me later that Steve ended up encouraging her rather than the other way around. "And don't feel down," he said. "Just keep praying and give Tami and Erica my love."

When I arrived at the hospital early Saturday Steve was already in surgery. Barbara was in the waiting room, her thoughts obviously elsewhere. I was thankful she wasn't alone; Sammy Mason sat nearby. If anyone could give Barbara the strength she needed during these anxious moments, it was Sammy.

Two hours passed before the doctor joined us. His expression was grim as he reported on the discovery of a massive tumor in Steve's right lung. Tissue from the tumor had been diagnosed as malignant. "It's a rare type of cancer called *mesothelioma*," he said darkly.

Barbara closed her eyes: she appeared about to collapse. Despite the devastating developments of the past few weeks, she had been sustained by hope and faith. Now this.

"I'm truly sorry," the doctor went on, "but you should know. It doesn't look good." He mentioned a possible link to asbestos inhalation as the cause. (Steve later admitted that following a driving mishap during the filming of *The War Lover* in 1963 he was urged to use more flameproof safety equipment. The asbestos padding he swathed himself in before each race shed fibers which he inhaled.)

Barbara began to tremble. Sammy and I helped her to a chair while the doctor stood helplessly by.

Surely something could be done for Steve. Great strides were being made in cancer treatment, new techniques had been tested and were proving effective. The doctor offered no words of encouragement, however, words we desperately longed to hear. I raised the question of additional surgery.

The man in white gently shook his head. "Steve's cancer is inoperable and untreatable by chemotherapy."

"Does Steve know?" Barbara asked.

The doctor nodded. "He also knows we'll do everything possible for him."

"How is he taking it?" she asked. "I mean, is he all right?"

"He was still somewhat groggy, so I can't be certain. He really didn't say much of anything."

"I've got to see him," Barbara said suddenly. She stood quickly and started to leave the waiting room.

The doctor called her back. Steve had just been taken from the operating room to recovery, he said. It would be several moments, at least, until the anesthetic wore off enough for her to go to him. Until then, perhaps she would rather wait in Steve's room upstairs. "It won't be long," he promised.

I volunteered to accompany Barbara. Sammy remained behind, alone for the moment with his thoughts and prayers.

The elevator took us to the eighth floor, its huge doors opening onto the long stretch of corridor that led to 8501. We walked like zombies, onward but without purpose. Our hearts and minds were numb.

At last we reached Steve's room. It was large and private, more like accommodations one would find in a hotel rather than a hospital. There were easy chairs and a sofa, where Barbara was spending her nights, end tables, lamps and a large television. Carpeting stretched from wall to wall and draperies revealed a picture view of the city. The only jarring note was Steve's empty bed.

Barbara slumped into a chair, staring quietly into space. She sat there for many minutes, unmoving, before she murmured, "Why does it have to be Steve?" Tears began filling her eyes.

"Don't give up, Barb," I said, moving to her side. "Steve's a fighter. He'll make it." The remark was as much for my benefit as for hers.

"I know," she said, the words sticking in her throat, "it's just . . . " She began sobbing openly, and I put my arm around her. She seemed so lost, so fragile.

It wasn't long before a nurse appeared to announce that Steve was asking for Barbara. She wiped her eyes and joined the woman, motioning for me to follow.

I waited outside the recovery room while Barbara went inside. Nearly an hour passed before I saw her again. Her eyes were downcast; she appeared drained and colorless. I was almost afraid to ask, "How is he?"

Barbara was noncommittal. But in a wisp of a voice, she managed to say, "He wants to see you, Grady." That was enough, just what I needed to hear. Steve must be doing all right, I told myself, or the doctors wouldn't allow him more company.

The recovery room was small and dimly lit. Steve spotted me as I neared his bed. He smiled and said in a groggy voice, "Hi, buddy."

His voice was weak, his eyes heavy-lidded; the effects of the anesthetic had yet to wear off completely. Several tubes were connected to his body and an IV line ran into his right arm. He looked so pitiful, my heart ached for him. I tried to return his smile as I greeted him and asked, "How are you feeling?"

Steve looked at me for a long moment without answering. When he finally spoke he avoided the question. "How are my planes doing?" he asked instead.

I was grateful for the change in subject. And relieved. At that moment, I didn't know how I would have reacted if he'd really leveled with me. "The planes are fine," I answered, "safe and sound."

"Well, take good care of them for me," he said slowly. "And have the Stearman ready to fly. I want to take it up when I get out of here."

"I'll have it ready whenever you say." I nodded hopefully but my expression betrayed me.

Steve reached for my hand. "Don't worry, Grady. I'll be all right. You'll see."

"I know. We're survivors, you and I. Just keep your faith in God."

"Judy called to let me know she was praying for me. I told her not to feel down, and not to cry because I'm at peace with myself." Steve squeezed my hand. "I'm telling you the same thing. Just keep your chin up—and keep on praying." Steve smiled gently and closed his eyes. He was growing tired. "I'd better get some rest now," he mumbled. Then he drifted off to sleep.

Barbara was waiting outside. "What do you think?" she asked anxiously. Her eyes were red.

Had she asked my opinion when I first saw Steve I wouldn't have offered much, if any, encouragement. But only a few minutes with him changed my mind. "I have a feeling he's going to be all right," I said. "Can you believe he gave *me* a pep talk? He's already making plans for when he gets home!"

"There's so much he wants to do."

"And he'll do it. I believe that, Barbara." She looked at me, still uncertain. "And what about you?" I asked. "You're the one who worries me now. Steve's going to need you."

"I'll be fine," she said. Then, "It's getting late. You've got a long drive ahead of you."

Where had the time gone? The morning, spent waiting and wondering, had seemed endless; the afternoon, all too fleeting. And there was still so much to do before returning to the ranch. Judy and the girls were eager to hear about Steve. We had made plans to have dinner together at the apartment in Fillmore. It was to be a special occasion to celebrate the positive news that I would surely carry back from the hospital.

The ranch house was all decked out for Christmas, just two days away. On the front door hung one of the many Della Robbia wreaths Steve had ordered from the Boys' Republic, a school for problem boys in nearby Chico. He had spent many months there as a teenager and had a soft spot in his heart for the place. The remaining wreaths were given as gifts to his friends at the Santa Paula airport.

Barbara had bought a magnificent tree earlier in the month, before Steve had even visited the doctor in Santa Paula, wanting to get a jump on the holidays. This was to be the best Christmas ever, their first in the new house, and the tree was a symbol not only of the glorious season but of their own joy and spirit, love and faith. Barbara thrilled in decorating it. She had even found special ornaments in the shape of small airplanes. "These are for my honey," she beamed with childlike enthusiasm, dangling the miniatures where they'd be seen against the fresh green boughs.

The tree stood next to the fireplace in the living room, its adorned tip nearly touching the high ceiling. Beneath the branches spread gaily wrapped and ribboned presents in bright colors of green and red, gold and silver. There were dozens of boxes in various sizes and shapes. But one gift was not there. As a surprise for Barbara, Steve had his longtime friend and mechanic, Sam Pierce, restore an old Indian Scout motorcycle. It was one of Steve's favorites, now to be hers alone.

During the afternoon of December 23, the day following Steve's exploratory surgery, the phone rang. It was Barbara. "Steve wants you to drop everything and come into town. Can you get away?" There was no urgency in her voice; it was simply a request. Steve was back in his room and feeling stronger, she said, and, as I soon learned, the purpose of the call was to have me transport their Christmas presents to the hospital. There was no hope of his being released in time to spend the holiday at home. "One other thing," Barbara said with a flurry, as if trying to sort the million and one thoughts on her mind. "Steve's been talking about his planes again. If there are any photos around, please bring them with you. He'd really appreciate it."

By the time I rounded up some snapshots and carefully loaded the Dodge van with Steve and Barbara's gifts, it was growing dark. At this time of day on winter Sundays, driving the freeways was usually a pleasure. No work or school traffic, no caravans of mountainous trucks, no knots of returning beachgoers. But something equally formidable had replaced them: holiday shoppers. There were long stretches of road where the traffic barely moved, and my progress was measured in inches. The minutes ticked away, turning a normal two-hour drive into three.

When at last I reached Steve's room the door was closed. Unable to knock, my arms loaded with presents, I tapped gently with the toe of my boot. When the door opened, Barbara stood facing me. "Sorry I'm late," I whispered. "Is he asleep?"

"No way," Barbara smiled, pulling me inside. "He's waiting for you."

Steve was sitting up in bed, watching television. He looked wonderful, rested, and quite hale, minus the tubes and paraphernalia that had engulfed him only the day before. I couldn't believe the positive change in him. Or in Barbara.

"Here comes Santa now," Steve said, flicking off the TV. "Sure was nice of you to come all the way down here and bring the gifts."

"My pleasure, but this is only a small part of it. There's still a whole van full downstairs." Barbara led me to the coffee table and cleared a spot.

Steve smiled. He was checking the delivery in an odd way, almost as if he were looking for something in particular.

"I'll help you bring the rest up, Grady," Barbara said. "No need for you to haul it all yourself."

I didn't mind, really, but I accepted her offer. It would give me a chance to be alone with her and there were questions on my mind, questions that couldn't be answered in front of Steve. Somehow, I had the feeling Barbara wanted to talk too.

As we turned to leave, I noticed that Steve was still preoccupied with the boxes on the table. Then I remembered. Reaching into my jacket, I pulled out the snapshots and handed them over. "Is this what you're looking for?"

Steve's big blue eyes lit up. He didn't say a word but the broad smile on his face told what he was thinking.

As it turned out, Barbara had nothing new to report. Steve's doctors had been in and out to check on him but they always left without offering encouragement. The prognosis they delivered following the exploratory surgery remained unchanged. Even so, Barbara admitted, Steve was feeling remarkably better. And for that fact alone, she and Steve were thankful and filled with hope.

It took two trips to the van before we completed the transfer of presents. Even without a tree and the usual holiday glitter, the display was awesome and I was reminded of a department store window I'd seen as a child. Even Barbara was impressed.

Steve paid no attention to our efforts. He was too preoccupied with his own project. He had cornered a nurse and had her busy taping the photos of his planes to the wall nearest his bed. He couldn't take his eyes from them. Again, he reminded me to have the Stearman ready to fly when he returned home. "I'm really looking forward to that," he said. Steve studied the pictures a moment longer, then asked, "Where are you spending your Christmas, Grady?"

"Well, I'll be at the ranch 'til afternoon, then drive into Fillmore."

Steve crinkled his face. "I feel guilty for keeping you away from your family so much. Especially now."

"Don't worry about it," I said. "We'll have some time together."

"Yeah, but not enough." Steve fell silent for several seconds, then, "Since Barbara and I won't be home, why don't you and Judy and the girls spend Christmas at the ranch? Everything's fixed up and I'd like you and your family to enjoy it. Make yourselves at home."

It was an intriguing idea and a thoughtful gesture, but I wouldn't commit myself without first checking with Judy. She had mentioned the possibility of her parents joining us, although nothing definite had been arranged. As it turned out, she and the girls jumped at Steve's invitation.

He had another surprise for me before I left the hospital that evening, and he waited until I was practically on my way before springing it. As Barbara was seeing me to the door, Steve said rather impishly, "Hey, Grady, you forgot something."

I turned to see him holding an envelope. He was pointing it in my direction.

"This is for you and Judy," Steve said. "Merry Christmas."

The envelope was stuffed full of money. I was too flabbergasted to count it on the spot but, from the markings on the top few bills, I had to be holding hundreds of dollars. Slightly embarrassed, I thanked him and said, "We have something for you too . . . but I'm afraid it'll have to wait until you get home. It doesn't travel too well."

Steve knew what I meant and his eyes lit up. His present was to be a big chocolate cake. Homemade. It wasn't an imposing gift—in terms of value it certainly didn't come close to the one he had just given Judy and me—but price was never a consideration to Steve and Barbara. They treasured the simple things that came from the home and the heart. And Steve, especially, loved Judy's chocolate cakes, even though he teased her unmercifully about them. The problem was, Judy did her baking in Fillmore. By the time I drove them over the rough roads to the ranch they tilted at an awkward angle. "I like cakes that look like old hats," Steve would say, "especially if they come from you, Judy. That's all right by me."

The following evening, Christmas Eve, Steve telephoned the ranch. "Are you and your family spending Christmas together like I told you?" he asked.

"We're all here," I said. "Presents under the tree and everything."

"Well, have yourselves the best Christmas . . . and give Judy and the girls my love."

"Will do," I promised. "And how are you feeling?"

"I'm doing fine," he said. "Don't worry about a thing. We'll be home by the end of the week."

Steve was true to his word. On Saturday, December 29, he and Barbara drove up the dirt road leading to the house and parked in the open area just outside the back door. As he stepped from the car he took a deep breath and grinned, as if to say, "Man, is it good to be home."

Getting to the airport was constantly on Steve's mind, but it was several days before he felt really strong enough to make the trip. Even then he wanted to wait until dark when there'd be fewer people around. For some reason, he didn't want to be seen. I learned why one night as he drove down a back road leading to the landing strip. "Have you seen these?" he asked, reaching into his pocket. He pulled out several recent newspaper clippings and handed them to me.

In the beam of a flashlight I read of Steve's stay in the hospital, and of a rare fungus infection discovered on one of his lungs. He had become ill earlier in the month, the articles stated, after developing a coughing and choking attack from inhaling dust during wild dirt bike rides in the desert. It was reported that Steve's condition worsened so rapidly that he collapsed, gasping for breath. They went on to say that "after first refusing to be hospitalized, he reluctantly yielded to Barbara's pleas. Tests have revealed nothing serious."

"This stuff isn't true," I said, dousing the light.

Steve grinned. "Yes, it is."

"What?"

"It's true as far as the public is concerned. It's what I want people to believe."

Steve fell silent for a moment as we approached the

airport; the turnoff to the hangar was just ahead.

"If anyone asks," he went on, "tell them I had bronchial pneumonia in my bad lung."

"But . . ."

"*Grady!*"

I nodded quietly.

Steve guided the pickup to the side of the hangar and shut off the motor. Then he turned to face me straight on. With narrowed eyes, he said, "I don't want anyone to know that I have cancer. Promise you won't say anything."

"I won't, Steve. You know you can trust me."

"And tell Judy too, please. I don't want any of this getting out. It could hurt too many people." Steve exited the pickup and slammed the door. "Besides, it's nobody's business."

We walked slowly toward the side door of the hangar. Steve said, "My agent wants me to do another movie. I told him to put it on the back burner for a while and I'd think about it. I don't think he'll be suspicious. I've gone for five or six years between pictures before. It's not like I'm bustin' to work all the time."

"If he's got a good script, why not read it?"

Steve snickered. "Let's face it, pal, I'm out of the picture business. I've done my last film. It's time for me to move over and make room for somebody else."

"Don't think about giving up, Steve."

"Hey, facts are facts. And remember what I told you. Nobody else is to know."

"It'll be our secret for as long as you want it to be." Steve gave me a pat on the back and we moved inside the hangar.

Seeing his planes the next day, Steve seemed like a different person. His expression lightened, even his stance. Every few feet he would stop to run his fingers along a wing tip or fuselage. The next day, at Steve's request, I pulled the Stearman outside. Then, with some help, he climbed into the cockpit.

"Are you sure you really want to do this, Steve?" I asked. "Maybe it's too soon."

He shrugged his shoulders and grinned. "I don't know. Maybe the FAA will get after me but I've got to give it a try."

I'd read about Steve's daredevil exploits on motorcycles and in race cars. Speed, he'd once admitted, was his cure-all. "It clears me out, burns away all the anger that's in my gut." I thought all that was behind him. At least, I'd hoped and prayed it was.

The propeller turned with a roar. "Be careful, Steve," I hollered.

The wind from the blades blew past his face. He smiled and signaled "OK."

I stood watching as the plane took off and Steve eased into his pattern, steady all the way. Then he headed east, toward the ranch and Fillmore. He'll be all right, I told myself. He's doing what he loves to do: *fly!*

Despite Steve's attempts to keep his illness quiet, word somehow got out. That fact hit home several days later as the blaring sound of an impatient horn summoned me to the gate. There, several reporters from one of the tabloids wasted no time in getting to the point, firing questions in rapid succession about Steve's illness. They had heard rumors, now they wanted facts.

"You're wasting your time," I told them. "Steve's doing fine."

"Is it true he has cancer?"

"I said he's fine!"

"Let him tell us. Come on, we want in."

"He's not here," I lied. "And you'd better clear the driveway before he gets home. You know how he feels about some of you guys." I swung the gate closed and hurried away.

Several days later reporters from the same publication called my wife in Fillmore and offered to take her to dinner. A substantial sum of money was also promised if she would provide them with details of Steve's condition.

Steve was furious. "Get your phone number changed *fast*," he fumed. "I'll pay for it."

The following day, as Steve and I were leaving for the airport, he noticed a car parked along South Mountain Road. Two men were hunched down inside. "See that car," Steve said. "Keep an eye on it. I'll bet it's those reporters."

As we passed the waiting vehicle, Steve hit the accelerator. A second later the car pulled onto the road in pursuit. But the chase was over before it had begun. Steve knew every back road and turn in town.

When we finally arrived at the airport, delayed only minutes, Steve was exhilarated. He had proven to himself that he hadn't lost his touch. He was as elusive as ever.

The incidents with the reporters didn't surprise Steve, nor did their tactics. It was only a matter of time, he figured, until the press became suspicious. "Let them grab at straws," he'd say. "They always have, where I'm concerned." What angered him most was the intrusion on his and Barbara's personal life, not to mention those closest to him. He'd come to Santa Paula to escape all that, and now it was starting again.

Steve kept a wary eye as he struggled to resume his life, one as normal as possible under the circumstances. On January 14, he and Barbara hired a housekeeper named Wilma Peele, a sweet, elderly workhorse of a woman with a delightful sense of humor. When she discovered Steve's love of antiques she quipped, "It's a good thing, 'cause he's got one working for him now."

That same day, Judy dropped by the ranch. The visit was unexpected but Barbara welcomed her with open arms and a big smile. "She was absolutely glowing," Judy remembered later, "talking a mile a minute and constantly waving her hands in my face." Judy didn't know what to make of Barbara's animated behavior until she saw the gold band on her wedding finger. "Barbara," she shrieked, "are you *married*?"

"No," Barbara answered, "but we're getting closer." Then she grinned self-consciously.

At the time, Barbara didn't know just how close she was. Two days later, on the afternoon of January 16, 1980 she became Mrs. Steve McQueen.

The wedding was informal, held in the living room of the ranch house. Steve had asked Sammy Mason and his wife, Wanda, to be witnesses at the brief double-ring ceremony performed by Dr. Leslie Miller of the Ventura Missionary Church. No one else was present.

It was up to me to keep people away. "I don't want anyone here when we get married," Steve had said earlier that day, "so stand guard. You never know who might have found out what'll be happening here . . . people like the press." He handed over one of his rifles, adding, "That should discourage any funny business."

For the occasion, Steve dressed casually in blue jeans, Nike tennis shoes and a long-sleeve sport shirt. Barbara wore a white pants suit with a small wreath of baby's breath as a crown atop her long, flowing hair. She carried a bouquet of daisies and baby's breath.

Judy arrived just as the ceremony ended and Steve waved us inside. "Well, we're married," he grinned, helping himself to some of Wilma's hors d'oeuvres and a soft drink from the small buffet set up in the dining room.

"How does it feel?" Judy asked.

"Great," he beamed. "Just great!"

I felt great, too. Steve's marrying Barbara was just one more evidence of how his life had changed since he became a Christian.

Chapter Four

The wedding made headlines. But the accompanying revelations were sketchy and brief, not surprising since the event was history by the time the papers were alerted. Follow-up attempts by reporters to get the colorful details readers hungered for went nowhere. Aside from the principals, only three people had been present at the ceremony—and they weren't talking. Steve and Barbara, except for occasional quick trips into Santa Paula, were content to remain behind the protective enclosure of the ranch. Incommunicado. There was no getaway honeymoon, not immediately. That would come later.

One morning, several weeks following the wedding, Steve decided enough time had elapsed to make a trip to the airport. The furor had calmed down, he felt safer. Besides, he wanted to see his planes. Only now it wasn't the Stearman that occupied his thoughts. The Pitcairn had been haunting him. It was the one plane that rattled Steve's confidence. Even after his successful solo flight in October, the Pitcairn remained a constant challenge.

One flight, in particular, had stayed with him. It was a near disaster. In taking the plane up, Steve almost dragged one of the wings along the runway. Had he not stabilized in time, the plane could have easily flipped over.

Now Steve was intent only on practicing his takeoffs and landings. But as he eased himself into the cockpit, uncharacteristically apprehensive, he bowed his head. I was reminded of a story Steve had told John Daly. As John remembered it:

"Steve had said one day, while Sammy Mason was teaching him to fly, that he was having a difficult time mastering his landings. Before he and Sammy took off that day Sammy said, 'Steve, let's pray that God helps you.' Steve replied that he felt he should pray only for the things in life like health, death, and those things. But Sammy explained that Jesus was much more personal than that, and insisted they bow their heads together and pray. After the prayer, Steve admitted that he had completed a landing that was so textbook perfect he had to concede that the Lord had just worked a miracle. Several months after that landing, when Steve was relating the story to me, the miracle was still fresh in his heart, and I could see that the joy of the Lord was really growing in his life."

Despite the few moments of silence, Steve appeared uncertain as he guided the plane forward, but after several practice runs he began to calm down. He seemed quite proud of himself when, at last, he returned to the hangar. Without removing his flight jacket, he headed straight for his favorite chair. "I'm a little tired," he said, settling back. "I'll take it up again after I've rested awhile." But Steve did not feel strong enough that day to risk a second flight.

He didn't know it then but he'd flown the Pitcairn for the last time.

The next day Steve was anxious to return to the airport. He mentioned nothing about flying or his planes along the way and, once there, he was attracted only to one of his old motorcycles. He stood over it for some time as if to reacquaint himself with a long lost friend, then walked it from the hangar. "I'm going for a ride," he announced matter-of-factly.

Barbara arrived in Cline as Steve climbed on the bike. She stood watching while he kicked and kicked, trying to turn the motor over. Nothing happened; there was no burst of sound, no sudden roar. Steve grew more frustrated by the second. "What's the problem?" Barbara hollered.

Steve looked up, disgusted. "The darn thing doesn't want to start," he bellowed. He kicked once again, then stopped suddenly. An intruder had caught his attention. A teenage boy, wandering by the side of the hangar.

The boy was no stranger to the area. He lived nearby and regularly jumped the chain link fence—Steve's fence—that cut off his shortcut home.

In a flash, Steve was off the motorcycle and in chase, easily catching up with the unsuspecting youngster. "What are you doing around here?" Steve shouted, angrily.

The boy stammered momentarily before managing to say, "I didn't do anything."

"That means *keep out!*" Steve growled, pointing to the fence. "You understand?"

The youngster nodded sheepishly.

"You sure?"

"Yes, sir."

Steve stared at his captive. "OK, then, go ahead . . . but don't come this way again, you hear?"

The boy didn't wait to answer before scurrying away.

When Steve returned to his motorcycle, Barbara and I were waiting for him. We had watched the brief encounter and overheard just enough of the one-sided exchange. "Honey, weren't you a little rough on the kid?" Barbara asked.

"I don't want anyone hanging around here," Steve mumbled, climbing back on the bike. Without pausing, he resumed his attempt to get it started.

"But, Steve," Barbara persisted, "he wasn't hurting anything."

The remark went unheard, or so it seemed, as Steve went on cranking. But he soon gave up. "Well, maybe I did put it to him a little hard," he said, a look of guilt crossing his face. "Which way did the kid go?"

"He's heading down the road by the freeway," Barbara said. "I can still see him."

Steve hurriedly climbed off the bike and ran after the boy. It wasn't much later that the two of them returned and went directly into the hangar where, for the next few hours, Steve showed off his prized possessions. The youngster may not have recognized the angry man with the beard who first chased him away, but by the time he left for home that day he not only had stars in his eyes but a few mementoes and an invitation to return.

The incident gave Steve a real lift. I wondered at the time if he would have been as forgiving under similar circumstances ten years earlier, or even the year before, when he first started coming to Santa Paula. He was still suspicious; he was always on guard, trusting very few people. But now, on the surface at least, he seemed to be less rigid and more easily reached. Steve was changing.

In early February, Steve and Barbara had a huge redwood hot tub installed at the ranch. It was set in the backyard just a short distance from the house. Surrounding it was a latticed enclosure, specially built for privacy and protection from the sharp valley sun. The tub was rarely used during the day, however, as the McQueens preferred the early hours of evening. It didn't matter that nighttime temperatures were often nippy, especially in the winter. The water, heated by solar panels on the garage roof, steamed at well over 100 degrees.

Unfortunately, their routine was short-lived. On the morning of Valentine's Day, a dark stretch of clouds moved in from the north and a gentle rain began to fall. By late afternoon, the showers turned into a downpour. No one had predicted the storm, one of the worst in Southern California history, and its force caught everyone by surprise.

At the ranch we kept hearing ominous news reports of mudslides and rising rivers but we felt safe under cover. It wasn't until I ventured outside to check on the animals that I knew we were in trouble. Cascading waters from the mountains above the ranch had choked the small drainage ditch bordering the east pasture, causing a break. The overflow was moving toward the house.

Although it was getting dark, Steve didn't think twice. "We'd better get to work before the whole thing goes," he said, reaching for his rain gear. By the time Barbara and I grabbed shovels he was out the door.

In the darkness, we stood ankle deep in churning water building a makeshift dike of mud. The current fought us constantly, eating away a good shovelful for each two we put in place, but finally the barrier seemed to be holding. "That should do it," Steve said, relieved. He leaned on his shovel and took several deep breaths. Then, "I don't know about you two but I'm soaked to the skin. Let's go sit by the stove in the tack room."

As we made our way back across the pasture, Steve checked the drainage channel nearest the house. It was much larger than the one we had just repaired but the water was rising rapidly. At one point, a small bridge leading to higher land crossed the channel. If the area under the bridge filled with debris, the water would surely detour toward the house. "We'd better keep our eyes on this one too," Steve said. "If it goes over we're really in trouble."

I started to laugh. "Why don't you call the tabloids," I said "and tell them you've got a hot exclusive—but they've got to send somebody out fast."

Steve chuckled. We both knew there was no way anybody could get to the ranch without a four-wheel drive pickup.

"I sure would like to see them come tearing out here for an interview with you and watch them hit all that mud and water."

"That *would* be funny," Steve said doubling with laughter.

Steve knew about my cousin, Danny, who had a bulldozer he used in his business. As we stood drying off by the heat of the stove, the rain pounding the wooden roof overhead, Steve voiced his concern. "Call Danny right away and have him check out the big ditch. He'll know what to do."

Danny and his brother Dean arrived a short time later, but it was too dark for them to see much of anything, let alone operate a bulldozer. He volunteered to return in the morning—if the lower road, the one across to the ranch, wasn't too flooded. I started to follow them out.

"Where do you think you're going?" Steve said.

"I want to get home while I can."

Steve furrowed his brow. "Are you nuts? You'll never make it in your van."

I started to argue but Steve retorted with his standard clincher. "You're staying here," he said. "And that's my last word on the matter."

I called Judy to let her know I wouldn't be returning to Fillmore that night.

By daybreak, the rain had subsided enough to give Barbara and me a chance to tend her animals. We had been outside only a few minutes when we heard a cracking sound followed by a tremendous rumble. At first we thought it to be thunder, but the roar continued—and it sounded nearby. We turned to find that a section of the mountain had broken away; chunks of earth and massive boulders were plummeting down the side. The sight was frightening enough, but what really caught our attention was the oddly shaped mound of rubble created by the slide. There, at the base of the mountain, we discovered a perfect cross. Like Jesus' cross. The formation was so huge that it was visible for miles and, later, people from town would ask us about it. When Steve saw what had happened he was deeply touched, believing that the slide was an act of God in more than the usual sense. From then on, he would proudly say, "My place is blessed."

The respite from the heavy rains was short-lived. Before Barbara and I had a chance to return to the house we were caught in another downpour, one that showed no signs of a break. Danny had yet to arrive and a quick call to his office revealed that he had been summoned to an emergency flood job. Steve grew anxious and suddenly depressed. "I've got to get away from here for a while," he announced. Before the hour was up, he and Barbara were on their way to Los Angeles in his four-wheel drive pickup truck.

In their absence the thing we feared most happened: the big ditch jammed with silt and debris, causing the waters to rechannel into the yard. By the time Steve and Barbara returned later in the day, hoping to find the situation improved, water was raging within two feet of the side porch. Boulders and mud, washed down from the mountain, were everywhere.

That night, as the rain continued, I volunteered to keep watch with a flashlight. It was too late to divert the water at this point but I could, at least, alert Steve and Barbara should evacuation be necessary. Luckily, it wasn't.

It would have been hard to imagine rain falling harder than it had during the night but with morning came a deluge. Sheets of water so dense that it was almost impossible to see. Another call to Danny brought good news. He was on his way.

Danny went right to work with his bulldozer, first pushing the mud toward the ranch house to form a dike, then opening the channel to divert the water back on its original course. He stayed on the job throughout the day, mindless of the driving rain and water that, in places, reached depths of several feet.

The storm raged on for yet another day, creating enormous problems throughout the area, but the ranch was saved. The once green and grassy land was a sea of mud and boulders, but that seemed unimportant. Once dry, the cleanup could begin.

As the last of the storm clouds disappeared, Steve received a phone call from his friend, carpenter John Daly. John remembers: "I was concerned about how the house had pulled through the torrential rains, at least that was my excuse for calling. I'd read about Steve's illness and while I'm not real good at talking to people about a terminal disease, I wanted to do what I could to encourage him in any way possible. He assured me that everything seemed fine."

Steve was hesitant to talk much about himself, John recalled, and the conversation was rather brief. But a week later they spoke again, this time at length. "At first Steve seemed to be hurrying through the small talk, but then he finally came out with what was really on his mind. He asked, 'John, how long do you think I should read my Bible every day?' Before I could answer, he went on, 'I've wanted to ask you what would be the best part for me to read right now. And I really want you to pray for me, OK?' I was really moved."

John Daly suggested that Steve read *John,* chapters 14-17. "He said he would and I discerned somewhere, probably deep in the tone of his voice, that the man who had made it to the top of this world was going to make it to the top of the next."

In late February, Steve returned to Cedars-Sinai Medical Center for more tests and examination. The medication he'd been taking since late December had accomplished nothing. There was no halt to the spread of his cancer, no hoped for regression. He was given two months, at most, to live. "I can't believe it's over," he said privately. "I *won't* believe it. There's so much I want to do, *have* to do."

Outwardly, Steve didn't appear too upset over the diagnosis. He continued to take his vitamins and medication and tried to live his life as usual. That included rising at daybreak to work around the ranch before heading to the airport, and attending church in Ventura on Sundays. There were good days and bad days, of course, the latter usually sparked by printed reports that centered on the failure of "frantic last-ditch efforts by doctors to halt McQueen's vicious and inoperable cancer."

The reports began circulating less than a week after Steve's visit to Cedars-Sinai and were credited to several unnamed sources, including a number of the hospital's pathology department and "a physician." The information, allegedly documented, was filled with inaccuracies and often was sensationalized. One publication devoted an entire page to "shocking revelations," one-fifth of which detailed how, in December, doctors had "implanted radioactive cobalt (which kills cancer cells) in McQueen's chest—right on the malignancy. They sewed him up, leaving the cobalt inside. Two months later," the report went on, "the superstar was back in the hospital. Doctors reopened his chest, removed the cobalt and found that it had failed miserably . . . They stitched him up again." The truth is, Steve never had cobalt implanted in his chest.

Although Steve's condition was general knowledge by now, he still refused to admit that he was ill when he was away from the ranch. And he never gave up hope. "I expect to win this battle," he said, "but no matter how it goes, I'm at peace with God. I can't lose." He also had a plan. He was to see another doctor, a specialist, in April. But that was nearly two months away.

On the morning of March 6, Steve and I went to the airport. He wanted to work on his toys; it was good therapy and he enjoyed puttering. I hadn't mentioned that it was my birthday. Knowing Steve, he'd want to go out of his way to do something, and there was no need for that.

Around noon, Barbara arrived. She was hungry, she said, and wanted to go out for lunch. Reluctantly, Steve agreed. As they turned to leave he turned back and said, "Come on, Grady, let's go eat."

I begged off. "Not today, Steve. I always go with the two of you—and there are times you should be alone together."

He stopped in his tracks. "Get in the truck," he said firmly, "and I mean it!"

We drove to the Old Gang Restaurant in Santa Paula so Steve could have burned halibut steak and mashed potatoes. The place was crowded but we got a table right away; the waitresses rarely kept Steve waiting.

Toward the end of the meal I heard a slight commotion

in the kitchen. I looked up to see a line of waitresses filing into the dining room. The leader carried a cake topped with burning candles, and the ladies were singing "Happy Birthday" at the top of their voices. To *me!* While I nearly slid under the table, Steve was grinning from ear to ear. It wasn't until he started laughing at my embarrassment that I realized who had tipped off the restaurant. He had known about March 6 all along—and he'd been counting the days.

I vowed to get even. Just when, I didn't know. Another birthday was coming up toward the end of the month: Steve's fiftieth. But that was too long to wait.

Within the week, Steve and Barbara left on a week-long trip up the coast. Barbara had accepted a modeling job and Steve wanted to be with her. On the way home they planned to scout the antique shops in Santa Barbara, turning the time away into a mini-vacation. *Seven days alone!* Suddenly my mind began formulating a plan for Steve's surprise. By the time he and Barbara returned, the mud flat in the backyard would be cleared, resloped and transformed into a garden paradise, complete with a wading pond. Time was short but I knew I could pull it off. I had to!

Chapter Five

Tom Horn, a motion picture co-starring Steve and Linda Evans (of *Big Valley* and *Dynasty* television fame), had been completed prior to the start of Steve's visits to Santa Paula in early 1979. He admitted that he hadn't wanted to do the movie when it was first offered to him, and did so only to fulfill a commitment. Now, in mid-March of 1980, he was eager to attend the premiere showing.

Steve was not one to socialize or even mingle in crowds. The party to celebrate his soloing the Pitcairn was an exception. Even that, despite his good intentions, ended abruptly because of his extreme discomfort. Only once before while in Santa Paula, not too many weeks following the Pitcairn party, had he accepted an invitation. The occasion was a barbecue at the airport. He hadn't really wanted to go and nearly didn't. *Jaws* was showing on television that night and he'd never seen the film. It wasn't until the movie ended that he and Barbara appeared, hours late. Of course, none of the guests had left, clinging to the hope that Steve McQueen would soon join them. But their patience was hardly rewarded. As much as Steve liked the townspeople, he could not bring himself to mix with them in such numbers. So he simply filled his plate and went off to a quiet corner where he could enjoy his meal without interruption. Although he had been labeled as withdrawn and a loner, he referred to himself as "an oblique person." He explained that as being "someone different."

The *Tom Horn* premiere was another matter. Steve felt his presence at the Mann Theater in nearby Oxnard was important. Promoting the picture was of little interest to him, but he was determined to show the press and public how well he looked. Being seen, appearing happy and healthy, would help dispel the many "rumors" that had been circulating with increasing frequency.

In Steve's eyes he had changed little over the past few years. Audiences, he knew, no longer expected to see the fiery young rebel with the boyish features. That look had faded long before, replaced by a rugged, craggy appearance that, if anything, enhanced his appeal. "I was never the pretty boy type anyway," he confessed. "If my face was my fortune I'd still be scamming for nickels and dimes."

To some extent, Steve was correct in his assumption. Those of us who saw him regularly failed to notice any change in his physical appearance. Perhaps he had lost some weight but the loss certainly hadn't been dramatic and wasn't clearly obvious.

Steve seemed somewhat apprehensive on the morning of the premiere. I arrived at the ranch to find him in the yard walking back and forth across the freshly rolled lawn, almost pacing. He said he was inspecting the new plantings, the shrubs and trees, and talked of stocking the wading pond with geese and swans for Barbara. Then, abruptly, his interest was elsewhere. "Let's get to the airport," he said, impatiently. "I want to take the Stearman up."

Normally, on arrival at the hangar, Steve had a routine. No matter what he had planned or what was on his mind, he would first spend some time, however brief, at his workbench with his collection of toys. On this morning, however, he had eyes only for one plane. "Help me push the Stearman outside," he said. "I want to refuel before I take off."

We guided the old yellow biplane to one of the gas pumps just beyond the hangar doors. As Steve climbed onto the fuselage to begin refueling, he spotted a stranger approaching on foot, a young man dressed in a bright red T-shirt and jeans. When the stranger was within several yards of the plane he stopped and stared. He had a smug look on his face.

Unlike the time with the teenage intruder, Steve said nothing. He simply stared back.

The stranger folded his arms across his chest and began smirking. Finally, he said in an evil way, "I'll bet your wife's real pretty, huh?"

Judging from Steve's expression, the remark and the man's tone of voice didn't sit well. But Steve kept his composure. Despite his rough exterior and screen image, he was a very sensitive man, gentle and kind. Only when someone—or something—riled him did he lose his temper. This seemed to be one of those times. I waited for the expletives to burst forth, but Steve fooled me. "Yeah, she's pretty," he said without blinking. Then, through gritted teeth: "And she's got a loaded .45 she uses on guys in red T-shirts."

The man looked as if he wanted to say something but

nothing came out. So he turned and walked away.

Steve grimaced and went back to refueling the Stearman. That done he eased into the open cockpit. "I think I'll head east for a while," he said. "I'll be back later this afternoon."

"Don't forget about tonight," I reminded.

Steve shot a knowing glance my way as he pulled down his goggles. "Oh, I've been meaning to give you something," he said, reaching into his jacket. He retrieved a folded slip of paper, smudged and dog-eared around the edges. "A friend from my racing days sent this to me. I want you to have it." He smiled then gunned the engine. Moments later he was airborne.

The paper contained a handwritten prayer:

> Lord, I pray as I race today,
> Keep me safe along the way,
> Not only me but others too
> As they perform the jobs they do.
> I know, God, that in a race,
> I the driver sets the pace.
> But in this race of life I pray,
> Help me, Lord, along the way.
> Although I know I am a sinner
> Help me to believe that with
> God you're always a winner.
> Amen.

When Steve returned to the airport that afternoon he was visibly upset. At first, I thought the stranger's remark about Barbara had finally gotten to him. But he acted more frustrated than angry, so it seemed only logical to assume that either he wasn't feeling well or he'd been dwelling on the evening's activities. With the big event only hours away it had to be a case of nerves. Steve once confessed:

"I get near suicidal when I see myself on the screen. I feel trapped and break into a cold sweat."

I didn't put my theory to the test. I'd learned never to ask questions when Steve was in a mood; far better to leave him alone to work things out for himself. As it turned out, he didn't need any prompting. He volunteered the information. "Remember several days back," he said, "when I went into town to pick up some things? The day I saw the old pump?" Steve didn't have to say more. The story came back fresh and clear.

On that day, Steve had discovered the old Union Oil Museum. The building itself, in the heart of Santa Paula, looks like a fortress from the Middle Ages, but housed inside is a historic collection of oil drilling equipment and related memorabilia. Steve couldn't resist the place so he parked and went inside. There he found a mint condition 1930s gasoline pump, the old style so common in early gas stations. From his description, it had to be a throwback to *The Grapes of Wrath* and "Dust Bowl" America, but Steve wanted it. He wanted it *very* badly. The pump was too fine to store in the hangar with the rest of his treasures, he said. It belonged in the living room at the ranch and he intended to have it for his own. He would have had it, too, except for a slight problem: the curator wouldn't sell the pump. Steve tried to persuade the man with great sums of money, continually topping his previous bids but money wasn't an issue. The pump simply wasn't for sale, not at any price.

Returning to the airport on the afternoon of the premiere, Steve had flown over downtown Santa Paula. More specifically, his flight pattern had taken him over the Union Oil Museum. Once again, he was reminded of his futile encounter with the curator. Not accustomed to rejection, Steve became upset. "I sure want that thing," he said doggedly, "and I intend to have it. One of these days I'm going back and change that guy's mind!" Today, the pump still stands on display at the museum.

Steve didn't want to arrive at the Mann Theater too early since his only purpose in going was to be seen, not trapped in lengthy interviews with reporters. He felt there would be a good crowd on hand outside the theater; the event had drawn considerable publicity in the local papers. Judy and I had looked forward to going and Steve didn't want us to miss any of the excitement so he suggested we go on ahead. "Barb and I will be along later," he said. "Don't worry if it looks like we're not coming. We'll be there."

The quiet town of Oxnard is not accustomed to being in the spotlight, but the boulevard in front of the theater was blazing like a Hollywood sound stage. Even the nighttime sky, crisscrossed with the broad beams of Kleig lights, was aglow. The marquee announced in big letters—STEVE MCQUEEN IN TOM HORN, while a smaller sign, posted at the box office, told hundreds of disappointed fans that the one performance was "Sold Out." Crowds lined both sides of the street angling for a view of the film's star as shiny limousines arrived and left. But Steve was not to be seen.

It was nearly eight o'clock, minutes before the screening was scheduled to start, when Steve's four-wheel pickup truck slowed to a stop in front of the theater. Wearing jeans, a dark sports shirt and leather jacket, he hurried from behind the wheel to Barbara's side. She too was dressed casually, in a tweed jacket, turtleneck sweater and jeans, her long hair falling over her shoulders. Before they could make a move they were mobbed.

Flashbulbs popped at close range and Steve held up a hand to ward off reporters. It didn't help. "Is it true?" they asked, jostling for position. "Do you rally have lung cancer?"

"I don't know where you get your information," Steve replied with a grin. He tried to push forward but the questions kept coming. Finally, he said, "Whatever you've heard is ridiculous, just rumors. Do I look like I have lung cancer?" Steve smiled and waved to the crowd. The reporters backed away, only to be replaced by a surge of fans. They swarmed around Steve like filings to a magnet, holding up pens and paper and firing questions. He stayed with them only a minute.

Steve fidgeted throughout the movie. He said later that he wasn't particularly pleased with the pace of the film or his performance, and watching his death scene on the screen had been upsetting. He and Barbara left before the closing credits, hoping to avoid another confrontation. But they were unable to escape unnoticed. Hundreds of people were patiently waiting outside the theater for another glimpse of the McQueens and, upon seeing them, converged quickly, yelling and screaming. Steve and Barbara made a run for the pickup. In a desperate attempt to get away, Steve nearly ran over a photographer.

The premiere proved to be emotionally exhausting for Steve. He did not set foot off the ranch for several days, opting instead to remain behind its protective barriers while he tried his hand at farm work. Steve had purchased a small Kubota tractor and was determined to master it while plowing under the weeds in the fields. But the man who at one time had placed second to Mario Andretti in the Sebring twelve-hour endurance test, and who had thrilled millions of moviegoers with his daring exploits, found the going rough. More often than not, he would abandon the machine in mid-field for less challenging chores.

By the end of the week, Steve was ready to brave the outside world once again, and he resumed his visits to the airport. There, each afternoon, he would sit outside his hangar chewing great wads of tobacco or beef jerky while watching the sky for takeoffs and landings. One day, three old Cadillacs converged upon him as he sat outside alone. Out stepped five long-haired young men, hippy types. They stayed only a short time and left almost as quickly as they'd appeared. No sooner had they gone when Steve hurried inside to track Judy and me down.

"Hey, want to hear a good one?" he chuckled. Without pausing he went on. "You'll never guess who I just talked to. Musicians. *Rock* musicians. And get this, they offered me twenty-five grand to appear in my next movie."

"What for?" I asked.

"Just to *be* in it!" he laughed. "They figured a shot with me would help get them noticed. I didn't believe them so they pulled out the cash on the spot."

"Not bad. What did you tell them?"

"The same old story—that I just finished *The Hunter* and I wasn't in any rush to get back to work."

Steve marked his fiftieth birthday on March 24 without much fanfare. All he wanted to do was have lunch at his favorite restaurant. "I've got a taste for some of their halibut steak," he said, smacking his lips.

That was fine with Barbara, and I certainly didn't have any objections. Setting up a surprise "singing salute" with the waitresses would be easy. But Steve was suspicious from the start. "I hope you two aren't up to anything," he said with narrowed eyes, "'cause I don't want any of it. No surprises, no scenes, OK?"

"You didn't mind a couple of weeks ago," I said.

"That was different."

"No it wasn't, honey," Barbara teased.

"I'm telling the waitress," I said.

Steve laughed nervously. "You'd better not!"

I raised my hand to attract her attention even though

she had her back turned.

Steve pulled it down quickly. "Don't you say anything!"

"No cake? No singing?" I asked.

Barbara feigned disappointment. "No happy birthday to Steve?"

Barbara and I looked at each other, trying not to break up with laughter. "If that's the way you want it," I said.

"That's the way I want it," Steve repeated. He stared at us for a moment then went back to eating, not really sure the matter was settled. In fact, throughout the balance of the meal he cautiously watched the door to the kitchen in case he had to make a fast exit.

That afternoon, I drove Steve back to the airport. The heavy meal, he said, had made him drowsy. All he wanted to do was sit and take it easy. "I might even doze off," he added with a yawn.

"Sounds like a good idea," I agreed. As I started to wander away he called me back.

"No, stick around. I'd like some company."

"You're the boss," I told him. "Besides, today's your day."

"Yeah, a landmark," he sighed, rolling his chair to a shady spot outside the hangar. It was a beautiful day, slightly cool but clear; not a cloud in the sky. "I sure don't feel any older," he said, settling down. "Hard to imagine all the stuff I've crowded into my years. Thank the Good Lord some of it's been good . . . real good."

I pulled up a chair and joined him. "Can't argue with that. You've just about had it all."

Steve laughed. "I don't know about *having* it all, but I sure have *done* it all. Good thing you didn't know me a couple of years ago. Man, I was a mess. Overweight, into drugs, booze, you name it. Seems like I've spent half my life getting into trouble and the other half trying to get out of it." Steve sighed again as his eyes scanned the horizon.

"I sure have memories of this area," he said. "With all the places I've been—Europe, Asia, Mexico—I keep coming back here."

Steve rarely talked about himself. In fact, at one point in his career his reticence had earned him a reputation for arrogance. But now, as his thoughts took him back in time, he began opening his heart. It was as if he had to talk, needed to talk. And talk he did.

"I'm an Indiana boy," he said, quietly remembering, "but I've never considered myself a Hoosier. When my dad took off right after I was born, Mom sent me to live with my granddad in Missouri. I never knew my dad but I've been told we were alike in many ways. He had a go-to-hell reckless streak too."

Steve said his father was also a flier, piloting rickety crates with joy sticks, back in the Lindy days. "He did barrel rolls and Immelmanns in circuses, and he barnstormed and hedgehopped wherever there was a buck to be made. When Mom tried to clip his wings, that was it. One story has it that he was killed in China back in 1939 while he was with Chennault's Flying Tigers. But I also heard he died in the arms of a lady friend."

Steve excused himself for a minute. When he returned he had a fresh package of chewing tobacco. He bit off a hunk and settled back down. "My granddad's the one who raised me, or tried to, while Mom was off in L.A. doing her thing. I had so many stepfathers I can't even remember all their names, and not one of them really cared whether I lived or died. I'm not making excuses but that's probably one reason I got so messed up. But Mom, she was wonderful, a good lady. The times we were together, she must have had it awful trying to control me."

At age fourteen, Steve said, one of his stepfathers had him committed to reform school, the Boys' Republic in Chino, California, after a run-in with the police. Steve ran away but was brought back and eventually settled down. There was a good side to it, he admitted. "The head man showed me what a little kindness was. He was more of a father to me than any man I knew."

Steve spoke without bitterness of his eighteen months at Boys' Republic. "Sometimes those days seem like yesterday. Then again I feel like old Father Time with years of wisdom and experience, and I want to go back and tell all those kids not to throw in the towel. I have gone back— until I got sick I'd go back two, three times a year—but I know they never believed me. They'd listen because they thought I was a big-shot movie cat. But they didn't really believe that the same thing could happen to them too. Now when I see some kid in trouble, I think, there but for the grace of God go I."

By the time Steve was released from reform school his mother was living in New York City. "She was going to get married again so she sent me the bread and I went across country. I got off the bus feeling like Li'l Abner. There I was in my big high shoes, Levi's and a Levi's jacket, a California tan and a square-cut haircut. I remember standing on 34th Street, and that was a bad looking crowd I was seeing." Steve didn't rejoin his mother, believing he had too much energy to be confined at home. Instead, he played poker for a living and "bummed around with a bad gang."

On the advice of a friend, Steve said he became a merchant seaman, but it was a distasteful experience. He jumped ship in the Dominican Republic and, to get money to return home, did odd jobs around a bawdyhouse, things like delivering groceries. With a twisted grin, he said, "I even got to sample some of the wares. The girls liked blond, blue-eyed men and they must have thought I was a stunner."

A few months after his seventeenth birthday, Steve

joined the Marines. It was in the service, he said, that he came to grips with the rootless yearnings that had driven him from place to place, job to job. "The Marines shaped me up, gave me discipline. Man, if it weren't for the Marines, I guess I'd have ended up in the clink somewhere." Part of that "shaping up," he admitted, included forty-one days in the brig for going AWOL.

After Steve got out of the service in April, 1950 he wound up in New York's Greenwich Village where he lived in a nineteen-dollar-a-month cold-water flat, repairing radios and TV sets by day and working as a bartender by night. He met a lot of girls in the bar, he said, but it only led to one- or two-night stands. "I knew I didn't want to get involved. It's the kiss of death for a guy to settle down to a pipe and slippers before he's sown his wild oats. Young years are for young things—like trying out your muscles with life. If a guy gives that up too early, something in his soul dies. Besides, love's a full-time job and you'd better play it by certain rules if you want it to work."

It was in the Village that Steve first came in contact with artists, actors, and writers. One of his acquaintances was a drama student who suggested he become an actor and offered to introduce him to Sanford Meisner, of the Neighborhood Playhouse acting school. "Meisner told me that if I stuck to a schedule of hard work I'd succeed as an actor. Well, I worked twice as hard as anybody." (The drama coach was later quoted as saying he was immediately impressed with young Steve McQueen. "Like Marilyn Monroe, he was both tough and childlike, as if he'd been through everything but still preserved a certain innocence.")

A GI loan helped pay for Steve's schooling but it wasn't enough, so he began drag racing motorcycles on Long Island for prize money. Soon he was hooked on this new diversion which not only brought in pocket money but offered the perfect escape from the rigorous hours and regimentation of drama school. "I came alive when I was racing," he said, adding, "the danger was seductive."

In 1952, Steve won a scholarship to the Uta Hagen-Herbert Berghof Dramatic School in Manhattan and soon landed a small role in *Peg O'My Heart* with former child star Margaret O'Brien. When he auditioned for the acclaimed New York Actor's Studio, run by the late Lee Strasberg, he won another scholarship. This association led to a series of summer stock performances, including a part in the national road company of *Time Out for Ginger* with Melvyn Douglas and, later, a crack at Broadway when Ben Gazzara backed out of *A Hatful of Rain.* By 1955, Steve had a solid background of credits.

"Do you remember *The Blob?*" Steve asked. Without waiting for an answer, he went on. "I look back now and I hate that movie. The producers said they'd pay me $3,000 to play the lead—or I could forget the $3,000 and collect royalties for as long as the film played. Well, the script was a real clinker and the money sounded good at the time so I grabbed the dough. I could kick myself now because it became one of those early sci-fi classics . . . and it's made millions."

Steve had admitted earlier to Judy that his early appearances in several "B" films did nothing to enhance his movie career. "TV gave me the big break," he said. He was being modest. As bounty hunter Josh Randall in the CBS western series *Wanted—Dead or Alive,* television made Steve McQueen a star.

He talked of his favorite pictures: *Nevada Smith, The Sand Pebbles, Papillon, The Towering Inferno.* But the one closest to his heart was *Junior Bonner,* the story of a former rodeo champion who lived out of step with the times—much like Steve.

"I don't know why I made it in pictures," Steve said. "I

never conformed with people's ideas of how an actor should behave or live. They called me 'Humphrey Bogart with spark plugs.' But I was lucky. I came along at a time when a guy could dress as he wanted, wear his hair as long as he wanted, and be as different as he wanted. If he could cut the mustard in a work bag, that's where it was.

"I knew I had something good going for me but I really had to work to keep it. A lot of folks got the wrong idea about how I got my breaks. I'm sure they think I just tough-guyed my way up to a studio boss and bullied myself into a part. No way. I worked hard, and if you work hard you get the goodies. I didn't wake up one morning and find it all spread out before me. I chipped off a chunk of myself with every role."

Steve drew in a deep breath, then slowly exhaled. He went on: "The movie business is tough. You take a man off the streets and make him famous and he loses all sense of values. That's why it's so important to have the right kind of friends . . . people who only like you for what you can deliver as a human being. And I'm not easy to make friends with. I've been labeled obnoxious, temperamental, irresponsible—all those things and some others too. Richard Crenna even thought the words I use are weird. He said talking to me was like talking to a Zulu warrior." Steve laughed.

"Well, a lot of stuff has been written about me over the years. Some of it's true and some of it's not. Good or bad it doesn't really matter. Things are different now, and I have Barbara to thank for that. Now I only want to be happy."

Steve pushed himself up from his chair. Standing, stretching, his eyes wandered across the sky. In a few minutes the sun would be setting. He had been reminiscing for hours. His words flowed nonstop. At last, he settled down again. "It's getting late," he told me. "You'd better go on home now."

I asked Steve if he wanted me to drive him back to the ranch.

"No, thanks," he said, and with a gentle smile he leaned his head back against the side of the hangar and closed his eyes.

I left Steve alone with his thoughts in the growing darkness.

Chapter Six

Steve hadn't been in a hit movie in six years, not since *The Towering Inferno* in 1974. His last picture, *An Enemy of the People*, had been a disaster. Adapted from the Henrik Ibsen play, a favorite of Steve's, it was to establish him at last as a serious actor, not just a cult hero. Steve's belief in the property and his own abilities was so strong that he undertook the filming through his own company, Solar Productions, at a cost of three million dollars.

Critics tore not only the film apart, but panned Steve's portrayal of the small-town doctor as well, saying he was "obviously miscast" and "unsuitable" for the role. After a series of limited screenings around the country, *An Enemy of the People* was shelved.

"What hurt most," Steve said, "was that I turned down work in pictures like *A Bridge Too Far* to work on

Enemy, and it cost me millions. I wish the public really had a chance to see the film and evaluate it themselves before being subjected to a lot of propaganda by the critics."

Although Steve wasn't high on *Tom Horn* he had hopes for the picture, and he wanted to do as much as possible to help insure its success. He couldn't handle a promotional tour but he was able to grant several interviews. Reporters jumped at the chance; it wasn't *Tom Horn* they wanted to discuss, however. The "rumors" about his health took precedence.

"The talk is," one writer said, "that you refuse to discuss your condition because of the possibility that backers may flee from your picture projects. True?"

"I've never been in better health," Steve steadfastly replied. "But whenever there's a rumor about someone being sick, in politics or business of any sort, it's bad for future plans to even try to explain. Of course people worry, they think it's a cover-up. Look what happens to the stock market when the President sneezes five times in a day. I'm in great shape!"

As for *Tom Horn,* Steve said, "It's not a new idea, but the script fascinated me, and the idea was one I could connect with today's high-powered business world. Horn is a gunslinger who is hired by a small town to protect them from the bad guys. He is totally used by his employers and is eventually framed for murder. It's very applicable to the way some people, especially in the film business and in politics, use people they feel are lower than they are, or 'unacceptable.' for anything more than a dirty job. It happens every day."

Generally panned by the critics, *Tom Horn* proved to be a box office disappointment. Even Steve was not spared. Wrote *Daily Variety,* " . . . he (McQueen) looks like he's walking through the part and the picture as a whole is such a technical embarrassment the rest of the credits must have walked with him."

Although Steve still refused to admit that he was ill, it was becoming impossible to hide the fact that something was wrong. By early April the forced "picture of health" look put on display at the premiere less than a month earlier had begun to diminish. He had grown thinner and the sparkle in his eyes had dimmed. Steve too began to notice even the most subtle changes in his appearance and he became increasingly self-conscious. In a desperate attempt to regain his lost weight, he gorged on starchy Mexican food. Whenever possible, he and Barbara would steal into town to the nearby Las Quince Letras Restaurant.

By now, Steve had stopped attending church. Except for those times when he was unavoidably out of town, such as on location shooting *The Hunter* or in Los Angeles undergoing tests and treatment, he had not missed a Sunday. He felt badly about not going; church had become such a vital part of his life. He longed to sit in his favorite balcony location again, removed from the congregation below but still as one with the worshipers in prayer. He missed joining in the reading of the Scriptures, and hearing the words of inspiration that seemed to nourish his days (more than he would ever express). But leaving the ranch had become difficult for him. Steve was never one to venture into public gatherings even in the best of health. And as the ravages of his illness became increasingly apparent, he could not summon the strength to make the trip to Ventura. Steve's ability to avoid the limelight, so uncharacteristic in his profession, had once been a strength. Now it had become a weakness. In spite of his forced withdrawal, he did not abandon his feelings for the church or his need for prayer. If anything, his moments of meditation increased as his need for God's love became even stronger.

Outwardly, Steve tried to give the impression that he was less concerned with himself than with others. He began showering attention on my daughter Erica, then six, who had been born with an inwardly turned eye. "We've got to get that fixed," he said. "I don't care what it costs, I'll pay for it."

An appointment was made with a specialist at the Jules Stein Eye Institute at UCLA and Judy drove Erica into Los Angeles. Following a lengthy examination, the doctor recommended that Erica wear a patch over her good eye to help strengthen the "lazy" one. We sighed with relief when we heard how simple it sounded. The word *operation* wasn't even mentioned. But getting Erica to wear the patch was a different matter. At her young age, she found it to be not only big and "ugly" but, worse, very irritating. She pulled at it constantly.

One day, following a visit to the doctor, Judy, Erica and Tami, our older daughter, stopped by the hangar on the way home. Steve wanted a report on Erica's progress.

"She won't wear the patch anymore," Judy said, almost in tears.

Steve walked slowly to where Erica was standing. Kneeling down, he pulled her close then cupped her small face in his hands. Gently he kissed her forehead and in a loving way said, "You'll wear the patch for Uncle Steve, won't you?"

Erica looked deep into Steve's eyes. Despite her pouting expression, she began nodding slowly. She worshiped him.

From that day on, Erica was no problem. The patch still bothered her but she rarely complained. And within two months she was able to discard it for good. While Steve tried to mask his own fears by diverting his attention to others, there were times when he found it impossible. Dying, he said late one afternoon in the tack room, held no fear for him. He had come to grips with that. "I've been sentenced and I can accept it." But the uncertainty of not knowing when and where it would happen gnawed at him.

"I think I know what you're going through," I told him.

"How could you!" he snapped. His eyes, wide and penetrating, bore down on me. Then suddenly his expression softened. "I'm sorry," he said, "I didn't mean that. I'd forgotten you're kind of in the same boat."

"Not really, but every once in a while I wonder when my heart's going to act up again. And if I'll be as lucky the next time."

"Does that scare you?"

"I try not to think about it. But if you want the truth, yeah, I'm afraid to die. But sometimes I wonder . . . well, what it's like on the other side."

"I've thought about that too," Steve said.

"I've heard stories about people crossing the line. Judy nearly died of pneumonia a few years back. She said it was the oddest feeling, like floating in space, but she could see a tunnel, a long corridor, and at the other end was a brilliant light, almost blinding. She knew that God was there, somewhere, waiting to take her hand. I like to think that she was looking into heaven and that it was all bright and glowing."

Steve didn't say a word. He seemed to be painting images in his mind and his mood was deepening.

"I wonder which one of us will be the first to know," I said cautiously.

Steve winced and shook his head.

Then he started to grin. If it took black humor to lighten his mood then so be it. "Remember how afraid I was when I thought I saw a ghost in the house that night?" I went on.

"No ghost stories, *please*," said Steve with a chuckle.

"The scary thing about ghosts is you never know who they are. But if . . . "

"I know, I know," Steve laughed.

"What?"

"If you knew that the ghost was me you wouldn't be afraid, right?"

"How'd you know?"

"Because if I ran into one and I knew it was you I wouldn't be afraid either." Steve grabbed my arm and squeezed. Then we collapsed against each other in hysterics.

Several days later Steve drove into town and returned in a new Volkswagen pickup truck. He was really proud of his new "wheels" as he'd had it specially equipped with an extra fifty-gallon fuel tank in the rear and a blower on the diesel engine. "This baby's supposed to get great mileage," he beamed. "It's got a range of over thirty-five hundred miles."

"That should get you back and forth to the airport a few times," I kidded. "Do you really need all that equipment?"

"Yeah," he answered, not explaining.

Not too many weeks before, Steve had been forced to borrow my old van because Barbara was using his Dodge. On his return that day he complained that the van didn't shift properly and that the motor was bad.

"It's an antique," I said, defensively.

"It's a junker," he corrected.

With the acquisition of the new VW pickup, I became the proud recipient of Steve's Dodge. "Drive it in good health," he said.

It wasn't much later that Steve announced that he and Barbara were driving up the coast to Washington. At first he said he wanted to test the new VW. Then he admitted that the trip was to be a honeymoon of sorts, the honeymoon he and Barbara had yet to take. "We'll be gone about a week," he said. "If you need us we'll be staying at the Davenport Hotel in Spokane."

It wasn't until Steve and Barbara returned that I learned the real reason for their trip north.

To Grady —
Thanks for all
your help Pushing
me in the air —
Steve McQueen
Santa Paula airport 79"

e, in the cockpit, ready for take-off. Summer 1979.

With Sammy Mason, Steve's flight instructor.

th Pete Mason following Steve's solo flight, May 1, 1979.

ve and his yellow Stearman biplane.

With me, Chuck Bail (back to camera) and Barbara outside the hangar, November 1979.

With actor Lee Majors at party celebrating Pitcairn solo flight.

ve and Barbara's Victorian-style ranch house in Santa Paula.
ow, the newly added porch outside master bedroom.

Two views inside the hangar showing Steve's collection of antique toys and motorcycles.

baseball team at Boy's Republic. Steve's in the back row, fourth from right.

he set of Le Mans, 1971.

Steve spent many chilly late afternoons around the old stove in the backy of his ranch.

The driveway at the back of the house.

e of Steve's favorite spots to relax—outside the hangar
nis old desk chair.

th Barbara and young fans on location in Chicago for *The Hunter*,
ptember 1979.

On the set of *The Hunter*.

...n me at the airport.

...y and Barbara at the ranch.

Steve, seated on his favorite Indian motorcycle beside his Stearman plane early December 1979.

Pitcairn biplane and The Indian Motorcycle with U.S. Mail sidecar.

e's old green pickup and a few of his antique gas pumps.

Old gas pumps and motorcycles.

Some of Steve's antique car collection.

ly and me.

Judy and our girls, Tami and Erica, with me at the hillside cross built in
Steve's honor.

Chapter Seven

Had there been an emergency during Steve and Barbara's absence, a quick call to the Davenport Hotel in Spokane would never have reached them. "We didn't stay long," Steve admitted on returning. "Some news people spotted Barb in the lobby so we checked out real fast." (According to a wire service report headlined, "Honeymooners Hunt for Haven," Actor Steve McQueen and his new wife, Barbara Minty, didn't get to enjoy their honeymoon at the Davenport Hotel in Spokane, Wash., very long. Hotel officials reported that the couple checked out—destination unknown—after Mrs. McQueen was spotted by a newspaper employee who recognized her and asked if she was the actor's wife. She confirmed the connection but said that her reclusive husband would probably refuse an interview. He did.) As it turned out, they hadn't planned on staying very long at the hotel anyway.

Their real destination was the remote area of Winthrop, Washington, not too many miles from the Canadian border. Despite Steve's earlier buildup, the trip was never intended to be a honeymoon, although the days on the road did afford him and Barbara some precious time alone together.

Steve had an appointment to meet with Dr. William Donald Kelley of the International Health Institute of Dallas, Texas, at Kelley's secluded 160-acre farm. Though not an M.D., Dr. Kelley advocated an approach to treating cancer through "non-specific metabolic therapy," which included a computerized program of diet, nutritional supplements, and "detoxification." Said Steve, "He treats the body that has the disease, not the disease that has the body."

In meeting with Steve, Dr. Kelley claimed that he was living testament to the merits of his unorthodox methods. In 1962, he boasted, he had cancer of the liver and pancreas and was given only eight weeks to live. "The man cured himself," Steve said. "by sticking to a strict diet of liver, pancreatic enzymes, exercise, and positive thinking."

Dr. Kelley offered Steve additional proof by claiming that his Dallas operation had programmed nutritional guidelines for some twenty thousand persons. Of those, he said, there had been a 15 to 20 percent cure rate for last-stage cancer victims and a 60 to 80 percent cure rate for those less seriously ill. According to Dr. Kelley, the institute's research met all the requirements of a science.

Steve did not travel north blindly. Quietly, as was his way, he had done some investigating. Steve was well aware, for example, that Dr. Kelley's training had not been in medicine but in orthodontistry, and that his license had been suspended in 1976 for five years after patients complained that he was more interested in treating other health problems than in straightening teeth. Steve knew that Dr. Kelley had been investigated by fifteen government agencies, including the IRS, the FBI, and the Food and Drug Administration; and that a book expounding Dr. Kelley's theories had been banned by a Texas court order in 1969 as "an unlawful effort to practice medicine." Steve knew the possible risks in contacting Dr. William Donald Kelley but, as he stated, "When you're in my shoes you'll grab at anything that's been known to work." Dr. Kelley gave Steve hope, an option he could not ignore.

When Steve and Barbara arrived home they brought with them box after box filled with plastic containers of vitamins, minerals, enzymes, proteins and other dietary factors. As Dr. Kelley's newest and most celebrated patient, Steve had been advised to take the dietary supplements in massive doses. He followed his instructions to the letter.

The meeting with Dr. Kelley and his wife, Suzi ("She gasped when she first saw me," Steve said, "and not from being star struck!") gave Steve new hope. Now it became easier for him to concentrate on the ranch, his pride and joy. There was still considerable work to be done. The huge, barn-like warehouse for his collection of vintage cars, abandoned during the heavy storm, was nearing completion. Two rustic archways, one with an electric gate leading to the house, were also in progress. Steve hovered over the workmen, inspecting their labors and prodding them to move faster. Even the slightest delays were annoying to him. He wanted to see results—and *now!*

All new construction had to pass Steve's tough test: "It's got to look like it's been here a hundred years," he said over and over again. Anything shiny, modern or plastic was unacceptable (he especially detested "cottage cheese" acoustical ceilings). If he couldn't have the real thing, he would create it—or recreate it with the strength, character and stability that only the years can bring. It was Steve's way of establishing the roots he never had. "I guess I'm trying to create my own pocket in time," he said, "not a movie set existence but the real thing."

To accomplish this, Steve wasn't against using a trick or two, including some movie magic. As the workmen put the last of the corrugated siding on the warehouse, Steve said, "I know a couple of guys at the studios who work in special effects. They can do anything, even make this metal look rusty, a hundred years old. They might even paint a few faded tobacco signs on the side of the building."

He had other ideas, too: "I'm going to put one of my antique gas pumps out in front," he said. "We'll have a tank put in the ground and fill it with diesel fuel for the tractor and the new pickup." And he wanted old railroad ties, not cement, for the driveways around the building. Within the week, three semi-truckloads of used railroad ties were delivered.

By early May of 1980, the ongoing work at the ranch was progressing so smoothly (or, as Steve put it, "under control enough") that he felt he could get away for a while. "Barb and I are taking a little trip," he confided one day. "You'll have to watch over things for me while I'm gone."

Steve was rather vague at first and I assumed he was again stealing away to visit Dr. Kelley at his farm in Washington.

"Not this time," Steve grinned. "This is going to be a real honeymoon. We're taking a cruise to Acapulco."

He sounded sincere and I wanted to believe him. Still, after the last "honeymoon," I had my doubts. It wasn't until he produced an official-looking document on Dr. Kelley's "Foundation of Life" letterhead that I knew he was telling the truth. Addressed to "Dear Customs Officers" and signed by Dr. W.D. Kelley, it stated in part: "This is to certify that Mr. Steve McQueen is a patient of ours who has been referred to us by his physician, Dr. Dwight L. McKee, for nutritional body chemistry balancing. It is necessary that Mr. McQueen follow a strict nutritional program . . . . The pills that he is carrying with him are all concentrated food supplements that are mandatory for his health program, and none of them are drugs or illegal substances. We would appreciate your expediting Mr. McQueen and his wife, Barbara, through customs without undue delay. If you have any questions in regard to these food supplements and Mr. McQueen's body chemistry balancing program, feel free to contact us . . . "

On the morning of departure a chauffeured Cadillac limousine arrived at the ranch to drive Steve and Barbara to San Pedro where they would board the *Pacific Princess,* TV's *Love Boat.* It was an uncharacteristic display of elegance for Steve, but then this was no ordinary excursion. It was to be special, crammed with memories to last a lifetime.

Once the luggage had been loaded into the trunk of the limo, Steve and Barbara appeared arm in arm like two newlyweds. I couldn't help but laugh. It wasn't the open display of affection, for that was their way. It was Steve's outfit. He had chosen to wear Bermuda shorts and a matching shirt, white deck shoes and a straw hat. He looked like a typical tourist; the only thing missing was a camera hanging around his neck.

He smiled awkwardly and offered his hand. "Take good care of things for me," he said. As he climbed into the big black car I was struck by how thin his legs had become. The sporty, abbreviated attire may have seemed like a good idea but it only accentuated his loss of weight.

Steve and Barbara were scheduled to be gone seven days. But before the week ended they were back at the ranch, rushed home from Acapulco by plane. "It was terrible," Steve groaned. "Barb and I both got sick." He blamed the rich food they'd eaten, and the water. "We thought we'd get over it but we didn't, so we hightailed it back."

Within days, detailed reports of the ill-fated honeymoon were hitting the newsstands. "The McQueens stayed inside Boat Deck Cabin 348 until the third day of the cruise," wrote one observer. "Only when the ship docked at Puerto Vallarta did the haggard actor emerge with his young wife. They were often spotted gazing at the ocean through their large cabin window, their arms linked lovingly around each other."

Wrote another: "The ailing superstar looked terribly ill. He rarely left his cabin and his bedside table was covered with bottles of pills left in plain sight. When the ship docked in Acapulco, the McQueens went directly to a private villa at one of the luxurious hotels where they remained in total seclusion."

With several days rest and Wilma's home cooking, Steve and Barbara were back on their feet. Once again, Steve turned his attention to the activities at hand. The newly completed storage building now posed a problem. The huge pull-up door, he discovered, was too heavy for him to lift by himself. He talked about installing an electric motor so that it would rise automatically. "I'm going to be weak for a while," he said, "and I'll need to open it without too much trouble."

Another concern was the poor TV reception at the ranch. Television had been good to Steve and he'd never forgotten; he could sit for hours, totally engrossed, before the set. He especially liked old black-and-white movies from the 1930s and 1940s: war movies, action films, musicals, almost anything from Hollywood's historic past. He had his contemporary favorites too, situation comedies like *Benson, Archie Bunker,* and *Sanford and Son.*

But watching television from his bedroom at the base of South Mountain, which interfered with reception, was chancy at best. On clear days he could receive only one or two channels and even then the quality of the picture was poor. Hooking up to a cable system was one solution, he thought, but the company was unable to run its lines out to the ranch. Without wasting more time, he contacted a firm in Atlanta, Georgia that manufactured satellite dishes. For nearly $15,000 he could have a twenty-five-foot diameter dish installed that picked up not only the networks but twenty-four other channels. He placed his order immediately. "It's going to be worth it," he said.

In early June, while the tabloids had Steve and Barbara planning a private South Pacific cruise in September (it was revealed that "McQueen had approached members of the *Pacific Princess'* crew during his recent Acapulco cruise and asked them to sail with him on a private chartered yacht"), Steve, urged by his doctors in one desperate last-ditch effort, traveled quietly to a parking lot in Los Angeles's San Fernando Valley where he began a series of intravenous injections.

"I'm not looking forward to this," Steve said grimly. "They're going to have me lying flat on my back six hours a day, five days a week for seven weeks while the medication drips into my veins."

It was to be a lengthy and arduous procedure and Steve demanded total privacy during the treatments. He would not travel to the hospital where other patients, visitors, and staff could stare at him. Nor would he be seen in a doctor's office. He was only agreeable to renting a fully equipped camper and having it set up in the parking area outside one of the medical facilities. There, with Barbara at his side, Steve began his agonizing ordeal under the sweltering Valley sun.

For the next two weeks, Steve and Barbara remained in Los Angeles. From then on they began returning to Santa Paula on weekends.

On Saturday morning, Steve cornered me, "I've got to talk to you," he said urgently. "Let's go into the big building." He was wearing his bathrobe and slippers. His hair was rumpled as if he'd just crawled from bed. His eyes were downcast; he appeared depleted and sullen.

We walked slowly toward the warehouse where Steve stored his vintage cars. Once inside he headed directly for his old Packard and sat in the backseat. I remained just outside by the running board.

Steve was silent for several moments as he toyed nervously with his scraggly beard. When he spoke, at last, the words didn't come easily. "I just want you to know," he began, his voice shaky, "if anything happens to me . . . " he paused, his eyes brimming with tears, ". . . if anything happens to me . . . you'll be taken care of . . . I mean you'll never—"

"Steve *don't*," I pleaded, interrupting him. I couldn't bear to hear the words or see the tortured look on his face. He seemed so depressed, so defeated.

"Let me finish," Steve said. "I've had a lot of time to think . . . and I've got to say this." He looked at me with troubled eyes as he drew a deep, uneven breath. "I've put you in my will, Grady, . . . and you'll never have to worry about money for your family again. You and Barbara . . . you're my life now . . . there's no one else I want to leave anything to. Barbara will get the ranch, if she wants to live here, and you . . . "

"No, Steve," I cried. "I don't want to hear any of this." I turned away and started running through rows of ancient cars. When I reached the open entry to the building I looked back and hollered, "I hope I never collect!" Then I ran to the tack room and shut myself inside. But I couldn't escape the sound of Steve's voice echoing in my mind.

Chapter Eight

Early Monday morning, Steve and Barbara left Santa Paula for the city to begin another week of injection treatments. Steve seemed anxious to "get on with it" despite the thought of spending endless hours within the cramped confines of the steamy camper. "The only way we're going to find out if this works," he said, "is to *do* it. I can't get on my high horse now. There just aren't that many choices left."

But Steve began to grow increasingly restless, and by late Thursday night he and Barbara were back at the ranch. He said he couldn't take another day in "the sweat box."

"The camper was driving Steve nuts," Barbara said. "First he got too hot, then he started feeling uneasy. We had to come home."

They arrived sometime after midnight. I'd been asleep for hours and hadn't heard the pickup pull into the driveway, but the dogs created a ruckus. Then the doorbell rang. "It's nothing serious," Steve said, trying to explain. "I just had to get away for a while. I'll be OK." With that he told me to get back to bed. "You've probably got a busy day ahead. You need your sleep."

Need it or not, sleep wouldn't come. For the balance of the night, I lay wide awake listening to Steve and Barbara as they moved in and out of the house, constantly on the go as if driven to ward off the endless days of confinement. It was dawn before they finally settled down behind the closed doors of their bedroom. When Barbara finally appeared that morning for a late breakfast she asked that any work scheduled around the house be kept to an absolute minimum at least while Steve was in bed. She was so concerned that any unnecessary or sudden noise might disturb him. But work had to be suspended for more than one day; Steve remained in bed through most of the weekend, resting and watching television.

By Monday morning, Steve was on his feet again and ready to go, determined this time to make it through a full week of treatments. "I've got to stick it out," he said stubbornly. "I've just got to."

He also decided to hire a dietician to cook special meals for his weekends at home. "There'll be a young lady coming in on Fridays," he said just before leaving for the city. "Be sure to let her in the house so she can use the kitchen."

The arrangement sounded simple enough: the dietician would stay only a few hours, just long enough to prepare Steve's food, then leave. But starting with her very first day on the job, her presence created a tense situation.

Wilma Peele, Steve's housekeeper, felt slighted at

having to share *her* kitchen with the newcomer. Until now, Wilma had done all the cooking at the ranch. Suddenly, she couldn't help but feel that the McQueens were not only dissatisfied with her work but that she was incapable of carrying out her duties without assistance. Wilma was so disconsolate by the time Steve and Barbara returned from Los Angeles on Friday evening that she could no longer hide her feelings.

She wanted to talk with Steve immediately. But seeing him enter the house looking so frail she didn't have the heart. So she stood by helplessly while he and Barbara went directly to their room. Dejected, Wilma was about to leave when Barbara reappeared.

"Steve's a little tired," Barbara said. "He wants to watch TV a while."

Wilma seized the opportunity. "I have to say something," she said quickly. Then, "Nobody's mentioned anything but I have a feeling you and Steve think I can't keep up with my work. And maybe you want someone younger to take my place around here."

Barbara didn't say a word. She simply turned on her heels and hurried back inside the bedroom. A moment later Steve was standing in the doorway, his brilliant blue eyes focusing on Wilma. "What's this I hear?" he asked. His tone was soft and gentle.

"Well, I—I—" Wilma stuttered, fidgeting with her apron. She looked ready to burst into tears.

Steve went to Wilma's side and took her hand. Then helped her to one of the chairs that circled the old dining room table and motioned for her to be seated. As he joined her he said, "Now, Wilma, don't you worry about a thing—not this house or somebody younger or anything. Just take your time and try not to worry, or work so hard." His expression turned serious. "I hope you're not thinking about leaving us."

"Oh, no," Wilma said, with a shake of her head, "but I thought that you and Barbara wanted . . . "

"*You're* the one we want and *need*," Steve said emphatically. "You're doing a wonderful job, and we're really very fond of you."

Wilma looked so relieved; she couldn't stop thanking Steve. But he had to do more than pacify her with words. He had to make certain she fully understood how irreplaceable she had become as a member of the household. The following week Wilma received a nice raise in pay.

By the latter part of July, Steve had undergone six weeks of treatment in the camper, with only one remaining. But the routine had become such an ordeal that he felt he could no longer continue, at least under the present setup. Steve had no intention of giving up the treatments, not now, not with only days to go, but he was adamant in expressing his belief that something had to be done to make the situation more bearable.

A week's stay in the hospital was the logical alternative but Steve wouldn't consider that. He wanted to be at home where he'd be more comfortable—and away from prying eyes. Since administering the medication was fairly routine, Steve won his point. With careful instruction, Barbara would be able to insert the IV needles into his arm.

In the camper behind the medical facility, professional assistance had always been a moment away. Now Barbara was completely on her own, and she never left Steve's side. Suddenly she became more than a loving wife and companion. She was Steve's doctor, nurse, right and left hand. Day after day, around the clock, she stood on call, never once complaining.

At week's end, one of Steve's doctors arrived at the ranch to examine his patient. But Steve required more than a routine going-over. Tests, including a lung tap, were vital to determine the success of the grueling seven-week ritual just concluded. Now it was imperative for Steve to return to the hospital. This time he didn't argue. He seemed relieved that this hurdle had been crossed, and he was anxious to hear the results. "I'll be back before you know it," he said optimistically, readying to leave. "This should be pretty cut-and-dried."

The following day, July 30, Steve called from Los Angeles to report. "Nothing's changed," he said hurriedly. "The cancer's not receding."

I wasn't certain I'd heard correctly, the words had come so quickly. Then he repeated himself and there was no misunderstanding. Despite the grim news, Steve didn't sound depressed or even angry. If anything, his voice was filled with determination.

I didn't know what to say except, "I'm sorry."

"Don't worry, Grady. This isn't the end of the line."

"Then you're staying in town for more treatments?"

"No," Steve said, suddenly talking in a whisper, "I'm getting out of here—and I need you to do me a favor."

"Anything, what?"

"Don't tell anybody what you're up to, OK?"

"You know I won't."

"Good," Steve said, "I want you to check out the silver Ford pickup, fill it with gas, and bring it to me here at Cedars."

"Sure, when?"

"Today, as soon as possible. We're ready to go now."

"What do you mean?"

"Just bring the pickup. You can drive Barbara's car back to the ranch. We're heading in the opposite direction."

"Where?"

"Mexico."

Mexico! What did Steve mean? My mind was crowded with strange thoughts, none of which made any sense at all. Perhaps, I rationalized, Steve was giving me credit for knowing more than I did. Perhaps, in his secretive way, he felt I would understand. I didn't, and he'd given me no chance to question him, for he'd clicked off before I could respond. Nor did I have a chance when I first saw him in his room at the hospital. Within seconds of my arrival, a nurse and two attendants were standing by with a wheelchair, ready to see him safely to the checkout area. It was as if they'd followed my shadow.

Steve said nothing during the elevator ride downstairs, even as we made our way through the crowded lobby and outside. He sat grim-faced, his jaw squarely set, his eyes fixed on some unknown spot in the distance. Few heads turned to glance at the frail, bearded man in the wheelchair. Those that did, failed to recognize the once familiar face. For the first time I noticed how much Steve had really changed.

As we neared the pickup, a woman ran to Steve's side. He turned to her and smiled weakly; it was his secretary. She had come from Solar Productions, Steve's film production company which he'd kept active, not too far away on Beverly Boulevard. He had called her from the hospital, Barbara said, to bring some papers he wanted. She was also to bring a supply of Veracruz cigars from the Tinder Box in Beverly Hills, one of the few places Steve had found that carried his particular brand. The cigars, however, were missing. His secretary had forgotten to buy them.

A simple oversight, perhaps, but Steve could not hide his anger. Nor would he leave the hospital grounds until the cigars were in his possession. At Steve's insistence, the woman would have to make a special trip into Beverly Hills.

Steve watched as she hurried through the parking lot to her car and drove off. With some remorse he said, "I shouldn't have done that, I guess, but when you ask some-body to do something . . . " His voice trailed off as he looked around. Barbara had wandered a few yards away to talk with several friends from the hospital, leaving Steve and me suddenly alone beside the pickup. I couldn't help but be thankful for the delay. It would give us time to talk.

"I have a few questions," I said.

Steve looked up from his wheelchair. "I was wondering when you were going to say something," he said. "I'm sorry but I couldn't explain on the phone." He glanced around again, then, "Remember that guy I told you about in Washington? Dr. Kelley?"

"Yes."

"Well, when I went to see him in April he was hiding out. He was in big trouble in this country. A lot of govern-mental agencies were investigating him, trying to shut him up. He told me there'd even been some attempts made on his life."

"Do you believe that?"

"Sure, why not? It makes sense. Think of all the com-panies pushing drugs on cancer victims, and all the doctors doing needless operations. Then this guy comes along who says he has a cure without drugs or operations. If he's right, and he seems to know what he's talking about, the people who call themselves experts could be made to look real funny."

"I understand, but what's that have to do with Mex-ico?"

Steve drew in a deep, troubled breath. "The doctors here say I'm a goner. They don't give me any hope. But Dr. Kelley does and he's the *only* one who does. That's why I'm going to Mexico. He's taken over a place called Plaza Santa Maria near Rosarito where he can treat his patients without any static."

Rosarito, Mexico; I had no idea where that was.

"It's not that far across the border," Steve said, "but it could be on the other side of the world and I'd still go. I figure I've got to try Dr. Kelley's approach. And if he can help me down there, and I survive this, I'm going to help him all I can. What I mean is, I'm going to get Dr. Kelley out of the woods . . . stand up for him and tell the world. If a *goner* can make it, anyone can. That should shut a lot of people up." Despite Steve's frail appearance, his eyes burned with fiery determination. And his voice was as strong, as unswerving, as ever.

"It's going to cost me a bundle down in Mexico," he went on, "but I'm lucky. Money's no problem like it is for an awful lot of sick people. They can't afford to do what I'm going to do, and I want this to work for them too. I'd like nothing better than to get Dr. Kelley's program legalized in the United States so that everyone who needs help can live. Being rich or poor shouldn't have anything to do with it."

Steve began to grow restless, eager to be on his way. Pushing himself from the wheelchair, he stood to scan the parking lot. He shook his head then asked to be helped into the pickup. I started to lead him to the passenger side but he wouldn't have it. "No, I'm driving," he insisted. Once inside, Steve checked to see that his and Barbara's luggage was secure. That done, he said, "We'll probably be gone a couple of months or so. Why don't you, Judy, and the girls move into the house? Might as well enjoy it."

A moment later, Steve's secretary arrived with his cigars. Then Barbara was seated beside him and the motor was running.

I wished them Godspeed as Steve held out his hand. I took it and held it tight for a long moment. Steve grinned. "It's OK," he reassured me. "Mexico and I are old friends. I've been there many times and it's been good to me." Slowly, he inched the pickup forward, then pulled away. All too soon, they were gone.

Before returning to Santa Paula I stopped by the apartment in Fillmore to see Judy. Her reaction to Steve's invitation didn't surprise me. Moving to the ranch, she felt, would be too hard on the children, uprooting them from their friends and activities. But she had no objection to my staying there; she insisted on it, in fact. "Steve and Barbara are counting on you to take care of things while they're away. We can't let them down, not now."

The thought of being separated from my family once again was painful, especially at this time.

"We'll be together," Judy said. "We'll see each other every day, I promise."

On August 1, two days after Steve departed for Mexico, *The Hunter,* his film that took him to the Midwest a year earlier, opened in Los Angeles. Although initial business was good, the reviews were generally unfavorable. The main problem, critics said, was not Steve's performance but his "annoyingly unrealized and childish on-screen character," a complete reversal of his usually strong screen image. With Steve's reputation as an excellent driver, particularly since the release of *Bullitt* in the late 1960s, his portrayal of real life bounty hunter Ralph "Papa" Thorson had him crashing stupidly into car after car throughout the film. *The Hunter,* most everyone agreed, was not what Steve's waiting fans wanted and expected to see.

Within days of Steve's arrival at Plaza Santa Maria he was making headlines again. The stories of his "flight for life" seemed incredible and, not having heard from Steve or Barbara, I didn't know what to believe. There were reports of his having fled to "a phony cancer clinic" and that he had willingly "put himself in the hands of quacks." There were stories describing his appearance. "I look like a survivor from Auschwitz," Steve was quoted as saying in an article that told his "once-rugged body has shrunk to 100 pounds, with a grotesquely bloated belly and pretzel-thin arms and legs."

How reporters learned of Steve's whereabouts, I didn't know. And so quickly. Whatever precautions he had taken to guard his secret had obviously backfired.

The answer came that same week. The news had come from Dr. Kelley himself. Within days of Steve's total commitment to his program, Dr. Kelley had arranged a press conference and a television appearance on Tom Snyder's *Tomorrow* Show. "It took Winston Churchill to popularize antibiotic medicine," the doctor had stated, referring to penicillin curing the English leader's pneumonia. "Steve McQueen will do the same for metabolic therapy."

"The operation is a fraud," a noted Mexican cancer specialist countered publicly. "Plaza Santa Maria is not a medical clinic. It is a giant con—a big money-making business run by con artists posing as cancer specialists. These people are using Steve McQueen to get worldwide publicity and money." Reportedly, the center had no lab, no x-ray equipment, and no clinical facilities.

The barrage continued. Dr. Rodrigo Rodriguez, who was credited as directly supervising Steve's treatment, issued a statement that Steve was on a daily regimen of saunas and enemas, shampoos and body massages as well as "image therapy," a controlled thought process that "wills the cancer to shrink." Said Dr. Rodriguez, "Mr. McQueen follows a metabolic nutrition diet involving more than 100 vitamin and mineral pills daily, enzyme injections and freshly squeezed juice from organically grown fruit and vegetables, raw certified milk and foods you would describe as 'health foods.'" The treatment reportedly was aimed at changing the patient's life-style and washing out the effects of chemotherapy and drugs given in traditional cancer treatment. It was emphasized that the treatment did not include the use of laetrile, the controversial cancer drug made from apricot pits, or the Maruyama vaccine from Japan.

But even Dr. Rodriguez came under fire. Although reports confirmed that he held a postgraduate degree in nuclear medicine from the University of Mexico, and had previously worked in a Tijuana laetrile clinic, he was regarded primarily as a radiologist (x-ray specialist). In fact, none of the Mexican or American doctors at the Plaza were considered to have had any real training in treating cancer.

A spokeswoman for the American Cancer Society called the treatment at the clinic "a hoax," adding: "This metabolic program is 180-degrees opposite what a cancer patient should get. There are dangers in the metabolic diet. It is not considered advisable." There were cries urging the public to beware, cautioning that some of the treatments used at the clinic could even be life threatening.

I hoped that Steve and Barbara were so isolated that they were unaware of the controversy raging about them. But Steve had entered Plaza Santa Maria with his eyes open, completely aware of Dr. William Donald Kelley's background. And he knew that the man's treatment contradicted all existing methods. As Steve said, the American doctors had given up on him. Only Dr. Kelley offered him hope.

In late August, Barbara phoned at last to report that she and Steve were doing fine, living together in a private bungalow at the Plaza, which was the custom for patients and their spouses. "We've been taking walks and reading and watching movie cassettes on the video machine," she said. "Oh, and guess what Steve did. He went over to the swimming pool here and jumped in. He said it felt great!"

Barbara's words came as a welcome surprise. "Then it's not true?" I said.

"I don't know what you've read," she said, "but probably not."

One of the reports told that she and Steve were virtual prisoners at the Plaza, noting that they left their quarters only at night because of Steve's "paranoia" at being seen. When I mentioned this to Barbara, she laughed.

"Steve isn't like that anymore," she said. "We've been doing a lot of praying. God has become a very real and personal part of our lives. Steve's definitely made his peace with God. He may have distrusted people before, but no more. His trust is totally with the Lord." Barbara paused a moment than said, "I guess you know why I'm calling. Steve wants to know how everything's going at home."

"No problems here. Just tell him not to worry about the ranch . . . and to keep fighting."

"Well, he's doing OK so far. He's not getting any worse and we're very thankful for that."

Barbara had another reason for calling. She admitted that Steve was not at all pleased with the food being served at the clinic. But he had received permission to have his personal dietician prepare special metabolic foods, in the proper prescribed quantities, and have them flown to Plaza Santa Maria once a week. Arrangements had already been made with pilots Art Rink and Pete Mason at Santa Paula Airport to fly the food to Brown's Field, near the California-Mexico border. A driver from the Plaza would be waiting to deliver the package to Steve. Would I, Barbara wanted to know, see that the food was ready every Monday and take it to Art and Pete at the airport. Would I!

From the start, Steve's weekly deliveries transported more than food across the border. There were also messages from home, stuffed into plastic ice cream containers, specially marked. It was the ideal way to communicate, much faster and more reliable than the mails.

One message, however, I couldn't send by air, yet it took precedence above all others. This one I had to deliver in person. It was from the Reverend Billy Graham. He wanted to arrange a meeting with Steve.

Chapter Nine

The call came from Hawaii. Billy Graham was in the midst of an international tour when he heard that Steve was anxious to speak with him. "I'll be here for several more weeks before going on to Tokyo," the famed evangelist said. "But I'll be in Burbank on October 31. If there's anything I can do before then, please call my office and they'll get in touch with me." Dr. Graham was not aware that Steve had gone to Mexico.

It was several days later that Barbara phoned again. "Steve wants you to come down this Sunday," she said, " . . . if you can get away."

She had to be joking. I'd have dropped everything to make the trip.

"Steve has a few requests," Barbara went on, "things he'd like you to bring with you." She read from a list: his flying helmet, goggles, and binoculars, photos of his planes and a set of knives, handmade by a friend. Gathering the items would be easy; waiting until Sunday, September 14, would seem endless.

On a plateau high above the rugged Pacific shores, several miles south of the seaside town of Rosarito, spread a cluster of single- and two-story buildings surrounded by trees and fences. At the main entry, almost church-like with its bell tower capping the arch, two uniformed guards stood before a closed gate. A sign spelled out PLAZA SANTA MARIA in bold letters.

I pulled my van up to the gate, letting the motor idle as the guards approached. They were big bruisers, extremely cautious with nervous eyes. "I'm here to see Don Schoonover," I said, following Barbara's instructions. Nothing seemed to click; neither of them spoke English. We stared at each other for several seconds then one of the men disappeared. He returned with still another guard, one apparently of higher rank.

"May I help you?" the new man asked. He spoke without any trace of an accent.

"I'm here to see Don Schoonover," I said again.

"Are you a reporter?"

"No."

"What's your name?"

I told him.

"Ah," he nodded. "Mr. McQueen said he was expecting you." The guard backed away and, with the wave of his hand, the gate swung aside. "Just follow the road ahead," he said, "then turn right. You'll see Mr. McQueen's car parked outside his bungalow."

Plaza Santa Maria was a sprawling complex. It was laid out like a rural subdivision but had the atmosphere of a country club, not surprising since only a year earlier it had been an exclusive oceanside tourist resort. Despite the brisk winds that swept in from the west, the narrow streets of cobblestone were immaculate. They were lined with rows of gleaming white cottages, converted mobile homes. Freshly manicured lawns, aprons of emerald green spread before each of the guest quarters, offered relief from the glaring sun.

Steve's silver Ford pickup sat idly in one of the driveways. As I parked my van, Barbara came running to greet me. She was all smiles.

"I'm so glad you're here," she beamed. "Steve's really been looking forward to today."

"How is everything?"

Barbara's smile faded. "Oh, we're all right," she said, shrugging slightly. She looked as if she wanted to say more. Then, excited again, she held out her hand. "Come on in, he's waiting for you."

I gathered the box containing Steve's things and began to follow Barbara up the walkway. As we neared the front door I suddenly became apprehensive. *How would I react to seeing Steve after so many weeks?* I wondered. Headlines flashed through my mind. Steve's shocking story had become such big news that scarcely a day passed without an update on his condition. Newspapers, radio, and television doted on him. It had become impossible to escape the outpouring. According to the latest reports, "The once rugged Steve McQueen has turned into a shriveled old man who walks with a stoop and has grown a long scraggly beard."

Barbara led me inside. Steve was sitting at a table in the living room. "Hi, pal," he grinned. "It sure is good to see you again."

We shook hands; his grip was strong. He appeared only slightly thinner than he had in August, but his stomach looked more bloated than I'd remembered.

"I can sit up like this for only about twenty minutes at a

time," he said, "then I get really tired and have to lie down awhile. But the doctors are really encouraged. They say my tumors are definitely shrinking."

Steve reached into the box I'd set before him and he pulled out his helmet and goggles. A broad smile spread across his face. "Boy, I'd really like to go back to Santa Paula and fly again," he said.

"You told me some good news," I said, "now I'll tell you some."

"What's that?"

"Billy Graham called."

Steve's eyes grew wide. "When?"

"Last week. He's in Hawaii and then he's going on to Japan. But he'll be back next month. He wants to see you."

"Oh, I've got to see him," Steve said urgently. "Promise you'll call him. Ask him if he'll come down here, and if he will, make all the arrangements. Rent a plane and come with him. *Bring him to see me.*" Steve leaned back and closed his eyes, as if to savor the prospect of meeting with Billy Graham.

Barbara put her hand on Steve's shoulder. "You probably should rest for awhile, honey," she said.

Steve nodded. "I am getting tired, but there's so much to talk about." He seemed to be having some difficulty breathing, a slight shortness of breath. He sat for a moment than started to get up. "Stick around a while, Grady," he said. "There's something I have to tell you."

Barbara helped Steve into his bedroom. When she returned she said, "Steve wants to see you now. He says it can't wait."

Steve was lying in bed. A large electric fan bathed him in swirling air. "Sit down," he said, patting the mattress, "here beside me. I've got something really important to say." He stared at the ceiling for a time, as if searching for the right words. Then, "The doctors tell me that Santa Paula will be a bad place for me to live. The problem is all the pesticide spraying that's done for the citrus trees. They said I'd have to find a place with cleaner air."

"You mean leave the ranch?"

"That's what I said when they told me. Santa Paula's my *home*. But they said it was either that or . . . well, I've given it some thought and I guess Idaho would be the best place."

"But aren't there other places—closer?"

"I guess but Barb and I both have some property in Idaho. And right now that'd be the easiest. It's nice up that way but . . . " Steve didn't complete his thought; it wasn't necessary. The ultimatum had obviously been devastating to him.

"What can I do to help?" I asked, almost begrudgingly. I wanted to try and keep him in Santa Paula but he didn't need any arguments at this point. He needed support.

"I want you and Judy to come with us. There are good schools there for your girls. I'll buy you a house . . . or I'll buy you some land and you can build a house. Do whatever's best."

"I don't know," I stammered. "You really caught me off guard."

"I know, but think about it. Take your time, talk it over with Judy and let me know. For now, though, I need you to check out something." As tired as Steve was, his mind was clicking at a fast pace. He wanted to know the elevation of Hailey Airport, a landing strip in central Idaho, to determine if his Stearman had enough power for takeoffs. "If it doesn't," he said, "find out what it will cost to install a 450 HP engine. Then get a camper shell put on my new VW pickup, and put antifreeze in all of the cars. Do you think I should sell the Pitcairn?"

"No," I said, "keep it."

"Well, maybe I should. But find out how much I can get for it in case I decide to sell. Go ahead and sell Barbara's Piper Cub and pack all my rifles and toys. Then call Idaho and tell the caretaker up there to make sure the house is ready to move into. I'll keep the hangar at Santa Paula but . . . well, sell the ranch if you can."

"Sell the ranch?"

Steve hesitated before answering. "Yeah," he sighed. "Barb and I talked it over. Do it before we change our minds." He sighed again and ran a hand across his forehead to wipe away the beads of perspiration. "Well, now I really do need some rest. I dreaded telling you all those things."

"I know," I said, trying to smile, "but don't worry, it'll all work out."

"I'm not worried," he said, "Everything will work out fine." He started to drift off to sleep but caught himself. "Hey, why don't you spend the night? It's getting late and there's plenty of room."

"I'd better get back," I said. "There's no one at the ranch, remember?"

"Yeah," he said softly, " . . . the ranch."

As I turned to leave he had one final reminder: "I'm still trying to keep things quiet, so be sure to watch what you say when you talk to people. I don't want anyone to know where I am."

Chapter Ten

"Is anybody home? Let me in!" The plea came from the back door. It was almost drowned out by incessant banging.

I hobbled through the house to see who was making the commotion. As I got closer I recognized the figure through the gauzy curtains at the window. It belonged to Barbara.

"Surprise!" she cried, rushing inside.

I lingered at the back stoop half expecting to see Steve. Barbara was alone. "What are you doing here?" I asked.

"I drove up to get some clothes and things," she said.

"Why didn't you let me know? I'd have brought some stuff down."

"You've got enough to do. Besides, I wanted to see

the animals and look around. And maybe unwind a little."

"How are things going?"

"Steve's doing great. He's going to make it, Grady, I *know* he is." She smiled thankfully then did a double take. "What happened to you?"

I was balancing on crutches, my left leg in a cast to the knee. "It's a long story. You don't want to hear about it."

"Tell me . . . what happened?"

It was almost too embarrassing to admit. "Remember that load of railroad ties Steve bought to use for the driveway to the new storage building?"

"Sure."

"Well, I dropped one on my foot."

"You didn't!"

"No, I'm just wearing this for effect," I said sarcastically.

Barbara looked sympathetic for a second then burst into laughter.

"Don't you have something to do?" I said, trying to change the subject. Surely, after the long drive from the clinic she'd want to rest. But Barbara was not one to sit idly by. She had something else on her mind.

"Help me get the dirt bike out," she said. "I want to take it with me when I go."

She was leaving the silver Ford pickup at the ranch and returning in the blue one. We started to roll the bike toward the vehicle when she suddenly climbed on and started revving the motor. For the balance of the afternoon, Barbara rode the hilly trails that bordered the ranch, often pushing herself at breakneck speeds. It appeared that the feel of power underfoot was now therapy for Barbara as it had been for Steve years earlier.

Barbara had originally intended to return to Mexico that same day, but she had exhausted herself and decided to wait until morning. That evening, following dinner, we sat quietly at the kitchen table. Time and again her eyes would wander about the room and, finding an object that stirred a memory, she would turn melancholy. She was particularly drawn to the art deco-framed posters from classic films that Steve had arranged on the walls, many of his favorites such as *The Maltese Falcon, Duck Soup, Dracula* and *The Wizard of Oz.* "I'm really going to miss this place," she sighed at one point. Then, "I'm almost afraid to ask if you've had any luck trying to sell it."

I hesitated answering. With all the other things Steve wanted done it would have been easy to say I hadn't had time. But that wasn't true.

Barbara seemed almost relieved. "I know it must be rough on you too," she said, "but Steve's going to want to know. And one of these days he'll be asking to see you again." She reminded me of that probability early the following morning before she departed.

Two days later, Barbara was on the phone from Mexico. "How's this Thursday?" she asked. "Will that give you time to do everything?"

I still hadn't called any real estate people, but how long would it take to make a few inquiries? "No problem," I replied.

"I told Steve about your foot," she said, "and he wants you to get the silver pickup serviced and bring that. You won't have to shift."

"Good thinking," I said. But at this late date I was more concerned about my report to Steve.

On Thursday, October 2, as I readied to leave for the clinic, a report on the radio caught my attention. All too briefly it told of Steve's request for privacy during his convalescence. The morning papers provided the specifics. "Hopefully, the cheap scandal sheets and curiosity seekers will not try to seek me out so I can continue my treatment," Steve had said. "I say to all my fans and all my friends, keep your fingers crossed and keep the good thoughts coming. All my love, and God bless you."

The main gate at Plaza Santa Maria was buzzing with reporters and photographers. Recognizing Steve's vehicle, they began closing in, firing questions in rapid succession. The friendly guard came to my rescue and, with the help of his subordinates, escorted me safely inside. "When did all that start?" I asked, relieved to be away from the rush.

"Earlier in the week," answered the guard. "One or two wasn't so bad, then when it got like this . . . " He shrugged his shoulders.

I thanked the man and started to drive on.

"No, wait!" he cried. "Mr. McQueen is no longer where you last saw him. He has moved to a new bungalow, one that is more secluded. The reporters, they hide in the hills with binoculars. They're everywhere."

The guard offered new instructions. I was to drive past the tennis courts for several hundred yards until I spotted Steve's blue pickup in a driveway. There I would be met by another guard.

The new man waved me down. "Park here," he ordered, guiding me behind Steve's blue truck. I slid from the driver's seat and pulled out my crutches. "I'm sorry," the guard said, "but you'll have to walk a few blocks. We're parking Mr. McQueen's cars here so the reporters won't know where he's living."

"Has anyone tried to get in?"

The guard pointed to a small hill less than a mile away. At its crest stood a replica of a Mayan statue. "There is a man, a photographer, at the base of the monument," he said. "He has a telephoto lens on his camera. We've been watching him all morning. There are others too. We've tried to run them off but they keep coming back."

Steve's new quarters were adjacent to the tennis courts, all but hidden under a canopy of trees. As I approached the bungalow I saw an unfamiliar face at the window, that of a young woman. She met me at the front door. "I'm Tina, one of Steve's nurses," she said. "I guess you're Grady."

"Yes, I am."

"Come on in," she said. "I've heard a lot about you. Barbara's still in bed. She didn't get much sleep last night but she should be up in a few minutes."

"Where's Steve?"

"He's having a treatment in his bedroom. It won't be much longer."

I sat in the living room and waited. It was a cheery room, spacious and comfortable with large sliding glass doors that opened onto a view of the mountains to the east, and the ocean to the west.

Barbara appeared within minutes from one of the back bedrooms. When she left the ranch after her surprise visit she was in a low mood. Now she appeared unusually perky, bright, and suspiciously inquisitive. "How's my little house?" she wanted to know. "And how are the animals? Is everything OK?" She didn't even give my foot a passing glance.

"Nothing's changed," I said. "Everything's the same as it was a few days ago."

"Wonderful, terrific!" she beamed. She all but bubbled.

"Do you have something to tell me?" I asked.

"Oh, no," she said, looking like the cat that swallowed the canary.

"What is it?"

"You'll see," she tittered.

At that moment another lady appeared. Her name was Annie. Like Tina, she was one of Steve's private nurses. They had been brought to Mexico by Dr. Kelley.

Seeing Annie, Barbara went directly to Steve's room. She was gone only seconds when Steve called my name.

I found him propped up in bed. The change in his appearance over the past few weeks was remarkable. Not only had he gained weight, most evident in his face and arms, but his stomach was reduced in size. He seemed pleased when I told him how well he looked.

Unfortunately he was unable to return the compliment. "Barbara told me about your little accident," he said, looking down at the cast. "I probably shouldn't have made you come all the way down here with your foot like that."

"What do you mean *make* me? Besides, I can get around as good as ever." With that, one of the crutches slipped out from under my arm.

Steve chuckled. "Pull up a chair and sit down. I've got some news for you." He turned serious for a moment. "Have you made any progress selling the ranch?"

"Well, no," I said, "but I . . . "

"What's wrong?"

"To tell you the truth, Steve, I haven't done a thing about that. It's not that I didn't have time, it's just that, well, something was holding me back."

"It's all right," he grinned, "don't worry about it. We're not going to be selling after all. The doctors told me yesterday that it won't hurt me to spend some time at the ranch, like a whole week every so often. That means we'll be splitting our time between Santa Paula and Idaho." Steve clasped his hands together in a thankful gesture, as if the reprieve came in answer to his prayers.

The change had Steve eagerly revising his plans. "When you get home," he said, "check some prices on fast planes with Turbo-charged engines, something like a Cessna 210. Since we'll be commuting, we might as well do it in a hurry. Time's too precious to me and I sure don't want to waste—"

Steve was interrupted by a uniformed security officer. The large open window by Steve's bed, he said, was on a direct line with a group of photographers who had moved into the nearby hills. "With their lenses," the officer said, "they can probably see you real good. I'm sorry but I'm going to have to pull your curtains."

Steve shrugged as his view disappeared. "I guess my request didn't do much good," he snapped.

It was time for Steve to rest; we would visit again, he said, later in the day. He promised the afternoon would be one to remember.

Tina and Annie were working in the kitchen. Barbara, they advised, had stepped out momentarily. I asked Annie if I could speak with her briefly. "Is it about Steve?" she asked.

"Yes. He's looking so much better. But how is he really doing."

"Oh, he *is* better," she said. "Definitely. Some of his tumors are way down in size. It's a slow process, but Dr. Kelley thinks Steve can recover completely."

"He's doing that well?"

"That's what the doctors say. But it's going to take some time. Steve's going to be here awhile . . . another four or five months, maybe longer. It's the tumor in his stomach that's going to take some time to treat."

The kitchen counters were stacked with containers of all sizes, each specially marked. "You're no stranger to Steve's diet," Annie smiled, since most of his food comes from his place in California. But there's something I'll bet you don't know about. Junk Food Day."

"It's something Steve started," Tina chimed in. "He got so tired of the food he was eating every day that he asked the doctors if he could get off his nutritional diet once in a while and eat whatever he wanted. They agreed to try it one Sunday and Steve got such a boost that now all the patients participate. And they love it!"

When Barbara returned she handed me a list of items that Steve had requested for the coming Sunday's Junk Food Day. It included eight orders of spareribs, ten hamburgers (with triple onions but no cheese), ten orders of French fries, twenty dollars' worth of beef jerky, one of Judy's chocolate cakes and a pan of her fudge.

Steve had more requests when he awakened from his nap. "Stop by my office," he said, "and pick up my movie cassettes of the *Thomas Crown Affair, Le Mans,* and *On Any Sunday.* I think the folks here might enjoy watching them. Oh, and ask Sam Pierce to get my Bandit bike mechanically fit. But be sure to tell him to leave it ratty looking."

"I have some papers for you to sign," I said. "I found a buyer for Barbara's Piper Cub. Or have you changed your mind about that now?"

He took the papers, glanced at the figures, and scribbled his name. He was so weak his signature was barely legible. "Have you heard from Billy Graham?" he asked.

"Not yet."

"Well, don't forget to call his office again when you get home. It's really important that we connect." Steve took a deep breath then said, "Now, there'll be some things going on around here this afternoon, as soon as a few people arrive. Stick around. I want you to hear what I have to say." A strange, intense look crossed his face as his mood darkened. Then, "You know, nobody on the outside really knows what's happening here. Or to me. I've been keeping quiet because I wanted to save my family and friends from some personal hurt and to hang onto my dignity since I thought, for sure, I was going to die. But while that was going on, certain people have been putting words in my mouth and it's gotten out of hand—and I don't like it. Well, it's time to change all that. It's time now to clear the air."

Around mid-afternoon, a crew from one of the Mexican news stations arrived with several small truckloads of recording equipment, which was set up on the lawn fronting Steve's bungalow. Only microphones were allowed inside, and what appeared to be miles of cable that ran through Steve's bedroom. He refused to be photographed; cameramen, all but drooling over the prospect of a photo session, had to be content with exterior shots of the bungalow.

Hardly anyone could have been disappointed with the events of the afternoon, however. Two separate statements were to be taped, rather than the expected one. The first, a brief message from Barbara, was read by Steve's agent:

"Steve's great wish is that the United States would allow the medical treatment he is undergoing in this country so we could go home and Steve could continue his program among the people and surroundings he loves. He has asked me to tell you, 'My body may be broken but my heart and my spirit are not.' He wants to thank the thousands of people who have sent their good thoughts and prayers, and hopes they will keep them coming."

The second statement came directly from Steve. "To the President of Mexico," he began, "and to the people of Mexico. Congratulations to your wonderful country on the magnificent work that the Mexican doctors, assisted by the American doctors, are doing at the Plaza Santa Maria hospital in helping in my recovery from cancer. Mexico is showing the world this new way of fighting cancer through nonspecific metabolic therapy. Again, congratulations— and thank you for helping to save my life. God bless you all . . . Steve McQueen"

As he signed off, a woman who worked for the news station monitoring the audio feed, crossed herself. She made no attempt to hide her tears. Others in the small crowd that had gathered nearby wept openly.

Steve had read his message in a slow, deliberate manner. Several reporters in attendance said they detected a shortness of breath in his delivery. Dr. McKee, who was now supervising Steve's treatment, later commented that Steve "was just too close to the microphone."

Barbara seemed genuinely pleased with the taping and relieved that it was over. Now, with Steve no longer denying his illness—or keeping silent about it—they could concentrate on the more important thing: getting Steve well.

Dr. Kelley substantiated Steve's beliefs. In a news release published on October 3, he stated: "We have been able to prolong the patient's life beyond earlier doctors' expectations. I believe that Mr. McQueen can fully recover and return to a normal life-style."

On Sunday, October 5, Steve was in a festive mood, even though he was going through what he called "my day for sickness." But he would not let a periodic low period get him down, especially on Junk Food Day. This was a special time, not unlike a carnival, where he could gorge on treats at will.

Prior to leaving for the Plaza, I had purchased coolers to transport the refrigerated foods, a portable oven for the ribs and hamburgers, and cake tins for the desserts. There were also several surprises in the bounty. Wanda Mason, Sammy's wife, and Wilma had each baked cakes for the occasion and I had picked a goodly supply of Steve's favorite Concord grapes from the ranch vines.

Despite not feeling well, Steve was like a youngster at the sight of so much food or, in his words, "real food." He could hardly contain himself; in fact, he didn't know where to start. So he sampled everything once then went back for more. To his amazement, he couldn't eat it all. Several cakes even went untouched.

Although Junk Food Day had been in effect for only weeks, it was customary for the patients—those who were able—to gather in the Plaza cafeteria where they could celebrate together. Steve had joined the others in the past but, on this particular day, he did not go. Still, he wanted to be remembered. Annie and Tina were asked to deliver the leftover cakes to the group with his compliments, which included an impromptu taped message and prayer. Steve said:

"I'm awful sorry that I won't be able to be with you on junk day today but, unfortunately, I'm not at my best right now. So I'm going to curl up here knowing that all the cakes 'n ice cream will be amply taken care of. I only warn you to take it easy on your eating so you don't become ill. In the meantime, if we could bow our heads and kind of make believe I'm there with you, I'd love to pray with you for a minute.

"We thank Thee, Lord, for all the kindness and understanding, and your special way that you reach out to all the staff, the doctors, the nurses, all the people who are helping us be healed here in this great, great experiment that we're all a part of. And for knowing in their times of anguish that you're there for them as they are very tired and overworked and need the Lord's love too.

"And for the patients, all of us who have cancer, in our times of anguish, and pain, knowing that the Lord Jesus Christ is there for us. All we need is faith and the ability to reach out, and to accept His love, cause He is there for us . . . Jesus Christ, our Saviour. Amen.

"Now, before everyone digs in for some ice cream and cake, I want to say have a real, real good time and I'll be up to see all the patients individually when I'm feeling a bit better. I'm sure looking forward to it, so have a nice time. Your friend, Steve McQueen."

As the day passed, Steve did begin to feel better. And

he was cheered by messages from friends at home. Lee Majors, Cliff Robertson, Pat Boone, and Chuck Norris sent their wishes as did Ray Stark, Kent McCord, Warren Cowans, and Nina Blanchard, Barbara's agent. Ralph Thorsen had called, and Mort Engelberg reported that *The Hunter* was doing good business around the country. Steve was genuinely touched by the outpouring of love and concern.

He talked of leasing his hangar at the airport and requested information from the Idaho Environmental Agency regarding toxins in the air. "I've heard there's an atomic waste dump somewhere in Idaho," he said. "Find out how far away it is from the ranch. I want to make sure it's not close enough to harm my breathing."

Word was received from the cafeteria that Wilma's cake, one of those delivered earlier, had been awarded a blue ribbon. "Be sure to tell her that she won a first prize," he beamed.

Steve never failed to ask about Billy Graham. "Have you checked with his office? Have they talked with him? Will he come see me?" He would not be assuaged until contact had been reestablished and a specific time arranged for a meeting.

By late afternoon, Steve was growing tired. He'd had a busy day but his outlook seemed stronger, more positive than ever. "I feel so much better about everything now," he said. "I really believe in this Kelley program and, now that I've turned my life over to the Lord, I sincerely believe I'm going to make it."

Steve's attitude was infectious, and as I left that day to return home I couldn't help feeling uplifted. The knot of reporters, photographers, and curiosity seekers hovering at the Plaza gate barely phased me. Nor was I annoyed when customs officers at the Tijuana border crossing pulled me aside for questioning. The empty containers that earlier carried Steve's food had aroused their suspicion.

From the start, their attitude was condemning. But they softened and their search was abandoned when I told them that they belonged to a sick friend, Steve McQueen. Suddenly their gruff expressions turned to concern. "How is Mr. McQueen doing these days?" they wanted to know.

A capsule report was all they needed and I was on my way. But several miles past the border I discovered that I was not alone.

On leaving Plaza Santa Maria, I thought I'd detected a car following me. But it had disappeared in the congestion at Tijuana. Now the car was on my tail again. I speeded up, it speeded up; I slowed down, it slowed down, always to remain within the same safe distance in the rearview mirror. It was impossible to see who was inside other than two men, the driver and a passenger.

Midway between San Diego and Los Angeles, the driver made his move. He pulled his vehicle beside the pickup and remained in the adjoining lane for several miles while he and the other man strained to see inside. Satisfied at last that I was alone, he raced on. *Were they expecting to find Steve being secreted to another hideaway?* I wondered.

For the next several weeks there were no calls from Mexico. Nor were there any messages of great importance to relay from Santa Paula, other than updates on arrangements for the planned move to Idaho which were included in the weekly food shipments. But reports on Steve's condition continued to flood the newspapers and airways. Dr. Rodriguez, the Plaza's medical director, issued a statement claiming that "Mr. McQueen has shown no new tumor growth, shows clear shrinkage of existing tumors, and has a much better appetite" than when he arrived in late July. While Dr. Rodriguez admitted that the cancer had, at one point, spread to Steve's neck and abdomen, "it is now retreating in response to treatment." He cautioned, however, that Steve was "a very restless man." He offered no answers when asked how that problem would be resolved during Steve's projected stay at Plaza Santa Maria, anticipated to be another two to three months.

On Wednesday, October 22, Steve's secretary phoned with word that Steve and Barbara would be returning to Santa Paula the following day. No explanation or details were given. "You'll have to make arrangements with a local supplier for oxygen," she said, "so Steve can continue his breathing treatments. But don't tell anyone who the equipment is for." The reminder wasn't really necessary. By now, working under wraps had become standard operating procedure.

Wilma arrived early the next morning to help get the house in order. There were windows to wash, floors to mop, bed linens to change. The pantry needed restocking with special foods. Moving from room to room—polishing this, straightening that—it seemed an endless task.

By midday, working at a feverish pace, the job was finally completed. Steve's rifles had even been unpacked, cleaned, and put on display in the wall rack over his bed. And to make the house appear more festive there were "Welcome Home" signs and colorful arrangements of freshly cut flowers from the garden scattered here and there.

That evening, Steve's secretary called again. "There's been a delay," she said, sounding rushed. "They've been detained another day. But they'll be arriving tomorrow sometime."

Sometime?

"That's all I know," she said. "But I must caution you not to tell a soul about this. No one is to know that Steve is leaving Plaza Santa Maria."

Chapter Eleven

On the afternoon of October 24, a Friday, Steve and Barbara arrived at the ranch from Mexico, accompanied by nurses Tina and Annie. Steve looked drained from the 250-plus-mile drive but he was in a playful mood. And independent. He insisted on walking from the driveway through the house to his bed without assistance. Only the cane he carried provided support, and he knew how to use it. As I stooped over to prepare one of his oxygen bottles, I felt a smack on my backside. I turned to find Steve with a big grin on his face. "It sure is good to be home," he chuckled.

Once settled, Steve began to talk about the reasons behind his sudden homecoming. "I haven't lost faith in Kelley or his program," he said, "not at all. Hey, according to the other doctors I shouldn't even be here now. Kelley's kept me going six times longer than anyone else said I ever would. But at the rate we're progressing it'll take forever to get rid of this thing in my stomach. And it's really starting to get to me."

Having the patience to wait for the bulge to shrink concerned Steve less than coping with the pain it created. The tumor was putting excessive pressure on an old back injury, making bed rest unbearable. He talked about the possibility of an operation to remove the tumor.

Everything possible was done to try to make Steve comfortable. But the weatherman didn't make the job any easier. Earlier in the week, gusty east winds began racing through the valley pushing temperatures near the 100-degree mark. The Victorian ranch house with its uninsulated walls and roof soon became a hotbox; even at night there was no relief. The old-fashioned ceiling fan directly over Steve's bed was an interesting and unusual relic but it did little more than stir the warm air. A large air conditioning unit was quickly installed in one of the bedroom windows.

On Steve's second night home a small brushfire, fanned by the strong east winds, erupted in the mountains directly above the ranch. The blaze quickly spread down the hillside only to burn itself out as it reached the open pastureland surrounding the house. The threat of danger passed quickly, but the air, filled with choking smoke and ash, was nearly impossible to breathe. Throughout the night and well into the next day, until the grimy pollutants settled, Steve was kept on oxygen.

Steve's breathing was a constant concern. No one talked about the possible dangers of pesticides in the area, they didn't have to; it was on everyone's mind. Barbara worried about how the trip home might have affected him. "I really floored it driving through L.A.," she said. "I didn't want him breathing that smog any longer than necessary."

A portable oxygen tank traveled with them to help Steve through such times.

At home, Tina and Annie saw to it that Steve never missed his breathing treatments. They watched him like hawks, forever monitoring his tanks, pressure gauges, and breathing mask. The oxygen bottles needed changing at regular intervals and a fresh supply had to be picked up each day from the emergency life support facility in Santa Paula.

Steve had been home nearly a week when Sam Pierce, his mechanic and motorcycle specialist, called with word that the sidecar Steve had ordered months earlier for his old Indian bike was finished and ready to be delivered. Sam apologized for having taken so long but the sidecar, or mail carrier as he called it, had to be entirely handcrafted since Steve had specified that it match his Pitcairn Mailwing biplane in color and design. "I can bring it over now so Steve can see it," Sam said eagerly, "or whenever he feels up to it. Just let me know."

It didn't matter that Sam knew Steve was home; he was a good and trusted friend. But I wondered how he found out.

"It's no secret around town," Sam said openly.

I invited him to the ranch. Sam arrived within the hour, anxious to show off his fine craftsmanship. But Steve sent word with Tina that he would see it later. The reason: he wasn't feeling well.

That wasn't entirely true. Had Steve felt better he still wouldn't have seen Sam. Steve wouldn't see anyone. No visitors, no guests. Away from the clinic, Steve was still extremely sensitive about his appearance, specifically his weight loss. His reaction to Sam's visit was predictable.

Sam must have been bitterly disappointed but he didn't say a word. Instead, he started the bike and let it idle. The motor seemed to purr, it ran so smoothly. Sam nodded, pleased with the results of his labors. "Well, I hope Steve at least got to hear how the old bike *sounds* now," he said.

Indeed, Steve had. He called it "a sweet sound . . . a healthy sound," and it rekindled his interest in returning to the hangar.

"One of these days, when I'm feeling a little stronger," Steve said, "I'd like to sneak over to the airport and go flying with Sammy Mason. But I don't want anybody to see me. We've got to go in the evening like we did before." Steve reached for several photos of his planes but lingered over them only briefly before setting them aside. They had suddenly become a poor substitute for the real thing. "I don't know," Steve sighed. "I want to do it but I'm so weak. I probably can't even get up on the wing to get in the plane."

"When you're ready to go flying," I said, "we'll get you up there, even if I have to lift you myself."

Steve's eyes danced as visions of soaring through the skies filled his thoughts. "It sounds tempting," he said wistfully. "Maybe in a couple of days."

By the following afternoon, Steve did feel well enough to want to soak in the hot tub. "I'd like to give it a try," he said. "It might be good for my back." He winced as he spoke, unable to get comfortable.

Steve walked from his bedroom to the latticed enclosure in the yard with the help of Tina and me, his spindly arms wrapped around our shoulders. I couldn't manage him alone as I was rather unsteady myself and walking with the aid of a cane; my cast had only recently been removed.

Once Steve was eased into the tub, Tina returned to the house. Lately, he had rarely been out of bed. This outing would give her and Annie some time to change his linens, plump the pillows, and straighten his room.

Steve settled into the churning waters until he was

chin deep. "Why didn't I think of this before?" he sighed. "This sure feels wonderful."

His eyes wandered about, as if he was seeing everything for the first time. The mountains, bathed in bright sunlight, showed the dark scars of the recent fire. Closer, behind a barrier of wire screening, Barbara's chickens pecked at the soil in search of food. He glanced toward the tack room and the driveway beyond. "I feel bad about old Sam," he said. "I hope he understands why I couldn't come out." Steve closed his eyes and sighed once more.

"Would you like to see what Sam brought over?" I asked.

"One of these days . . . when I feel a bit better."

"No, I mean *now*."

Steve smiled weakly. "I'll let you know when I'm ready."

"Stay put," I said. "I'll be right back." I left Steve's side, moving at a pace I hadn't thought possible with my bum foot. A moment later I was wheeling the Indian bike and sidecar onto the lawn beside the hot tub.

When Steve saw what was coming his eyes lit up. "Boy, what a beauty!" he said. "Sam sure did a good job."

"What do you think of the color? Sam said it matches the green of the Pitcairn to a tee."

Steve leaned forward to get a closer look, then said, "Turn it around so I can see the other side."

I swung the bike around to give Steve another view. He caressed it with his eyes, not missing an inch. He was overjoyed.

"When I get well," Steve said, "you can drive it and I'll ride in the sidecar."

"What are you talking about? You'll be hauling *me* around!"

Steve raised an eyebrow, then grinned. "I like your way better," he said.

That evening as I was leaving for home I found Barbara alone in the kitchen. She was furious and hurt. "Look at this trash," she said, pushing an article in my face. It had been torn from one of the supermarket tabloids.

I mumbled the headline: *Steve McQueen's tender gift of love for his wife.* "What's this all about?"

"Read on," she fumed.

The story told in detail how Steve, "frightened that he would leave his young wife alone and childless," had left a sample of his sperm to be used after his death in a "heart-breaking attempt to help wife Barbara Minty accept the shattering news that he was dying from a rare form of cancer."

According to the article, Steve had gone to a California sperm bank after a tearful talk with Barbara because he was afraid his harsh treatments would rob him of the ability to "make their dearest wish come true—to create a child as their symbol of love." Friends reportedly said that Steve wanted Barbara to have his baby as a cherished remembrance.

Had Steve seen the item in the paper? No. Certainly not. *Never!*

There was more. Officials at the sperm bank said they had instituted special security measures to make sure the sample was protected, "fearing that some deranged fan will try to lift it. There must be thousands of women who would love to have Steve's child."

Through all the months of uncertainty, Barbara had been so strong. Now she seemed near the breaking point. "Why do they have to make things up?" she said, near tears. "It isn't fair—it just isn't fair." Barbara fell silent for a moment. She looked so helpless, so vulnerable. Then, suddenly, she straightened as if renewed by some inner voice or power. "I'll be all right," she smiled. "What's that old saying, 'Sticks and stones . . . '?"

The article wasn't the first on the subject. Shortly after Barbara's marriage to Steve, rumors surfaced that she was pregnant. The baby, according to reports, was due "sometime in the fall." A short time later, however, retractions confirmed that "the news of his deadly illness have slashed all plans for a hopeful family and future."

For days, Steve had been looking forward to Thursday, October 30. It was to be a milestone, of sorts, the last day of waiting before he'd be talking with Billy Graham. Though no confirmation had been received from the Reverend's office as to his definite return from Japan, Steve had every reason to believe he would hear as promised. "He's got to come back on time," Steve said. "I've just got to see him."

October 30 was important for another reason. Steve had circled that date as Junk Food Day, his first at home, and to prepare he spent many thoughtful moments compiling a list of favorite food items. From the local Chinese restaurant he wanted two orders of almond duck, three orders of spareribs, chicken fried rice, sweet and sour pork and, without fail, a pair of chopsticks. From the delicatessen he requested an order of lean roast beef on rye bread, potato salad, Kosher pickles, cole slaw, a side order of Russian dressing, a carton of freshly squeezed orange juice, and three bottles of creme soda.

Steve spent the entire afternoon and early evening picking and sampling, stopping for brief periods to rest, then starting in again. Junk Food Day certainly buoyed Steve's spirits; he enjoyed his treats immensely.

It was growing dark when I stopped by Steve's room to replace his oxygen tanks. He was watching television but he was still surrounded by food, much of it cold by now. He didn't seem to care; from the expression on his face he was still relishing every bite. Working beside Steve's bed, I sensed his eyes burning into my back.

When I looked over my shoulder he was staring at me. I asked, "Is something wrong?"

"What's this I hear about you working late every night?" he said.

While Steve was in Mexico I had begun painting the inside of his hangar; the barn-like walls were in sorry shape and needed freshening. It was to be a surprise, and at that point I felt I had plenty of time to complete the job before he'd be home when he'd surely want to visit the place. But his early arrival meant stepping up the pace. "What do you mean?" I asked innocently.

"Don't give me that," Steve snapped. "Just because I'm holed up here doesn't mean I don't know what's going on."

"You mean the hangar?"

"There's something *else*?"

"No," I said meekly.

Steve reached for my arm and held on. "Look," he said, "I know what you're trying to do, and I really appreciate it, believe me. But you're making me worry. You've already had one heart attack and there's no reason to risk having another. It's just not worth it."

"It's not as bad as you think, Steve," I said, defensively. "A few hours every so often won't—"

"No!" he interrupted. "I don't want any excuses. I want you to promise me you'll cut down."

"But there's still—"

"Do what you have to do during the day but no more night work. I'm not being ungrateful, just selfish. What would I do if something happened to you?" Steve stared at me for a long moment waiting for an answer. Hearing nothing, he said, "Now promise me you'll cut down."

I promised. But the words choked in my throat as I watched this man, struggling so desperately for his own life, showing such concern for mine.

A few minutes later, Tina stopped me as I was leaving for home. "Don't forget we're having visitors in the morning," she said, lowering her voice. "Steve's doctors from the Plaza."

Chapter Twelve

Unseasonably warm weather continued as east winds swept across the flat valley floor toward the open waters of the Pacific. The winds had returned during the night, clearing the skies to an incredible blue. Now, as the sun began its upward climb, unrecognizable children frolicked on their way to school. They were dressed in bizarre costumes, their little faces all but hidden under masks and makeup and fright wigs. It was Halloween Day, 1980.

Dr. Kelley and his newly appointed director of Plaza Santa Maria, Dr. Dwight McKee, were waiting when I arrived at the Mountain View Motel in Santa Paula shortly before 9:00 A.M. I had never met the controversial Dr. Kelley before. A man in his mid-fifties, he was almost grotesquely thin with sharp, angular facial features framed by soft gray hair and dark, bushy brows that arched over penetrating eyes. He seemed pleasant enough, though some-what high-strung.

With the two men were Dr. Cesar Santos Vargas and his wife. Dr. Santos Vargas was introduced as a famed Mexican surgeon and frequent consultant to American doctors.

The visitors opted not to be driven to the ranch. They had their own rented car and preferred to follow as I led the way. On arrival, the doctors were escorted directly to Steve's bedroom where they remained sequestered until mid-afternoon. All but Dr. McKee, who wanted to remain at the ranch, returned immediately to the motel.

No sooner had the doctors and Mrs. Santos Vargas left than Steve began repeatedly calling my name. From the tone of his voice, it was more a command than a request to appear. Tina, hearing Steve's urgent cries, raced into his room with me.

Steve was sitting up in bed, a scowl frozen on his face. "I'm suffocating in here," he bellowed, looking directly at Tina. "You'd think by now you'd know how to work the air conditioner so I wouldn't have to swelter."

"But I turned it on high this morning," Tina said, sounding a little confused.

"Well, not high enough," Steve barked. "Show her how it works, Grady."

Tina and I marched over to the window unit for a close inspection. There was no need to fidget with any of the dials. They had all been set perfectly. I looked at Tina, shrugged, then turned to Steve. "Everything seems OK," I said.

Cleared of any wrongdoing, Tina marched from the room. I started to follow when Steve whispered, "Grady, come here." His expression was so intense I thought something might be seriously wrong.

"What is it, Steve?"

"Come closer," he whispered.

Now I *knew* something was wrong. I stooped by the side of his bed, very close to him.

"I'm sorry," he said, his voice still hushed, "but I didn't know how else to get rid of her."

"Why, what's wrong?"

"Nothing's wrong," he said, still looking serious, "I just want you to do something important . . . and I don't want the nurses to know. They'd scalp me."

"Oh?" I said, suspiciously. "What's so important?"

"Listen," he said, pulling me even closer, "go up to Baskin Robbins and get me a pint of vanilla ice cream with lots of chocolate sauce and nuts."

"What?"

"Bring it back in a plain paper bag, not one of those pink and brown things they usually hand out. That'd be a dead giveaway."

"I can't do that."

"Sure you can. It's OK, I do it all the time."

"Then why are we whispering?"

"Because I don't want the nurses to know. They think I should stick to my diet when it isn't Junk Food Day. But the doctors said ice cream's all right. It's energy food."

"You're conning me," I said, pulling away.

"No, listen, I need it. I'm burning up." The room wasn't uncomfortably warm, and his forehead felt normal to the touch. "Come on, get going!" he prodded.

"Well . . . "

"When you come back, sneak around to the side porch so you won't have to go through the house. I'll leave my doors unlocked for you."

Against my better judgment I left for the ice cream store in town. On my return, Barbara was standing at the front gate with a nondescript little man. They appeared to be pushing one another, and arguing. "Help me get rid of this guy," Barbara called out. "He won't leave."

I jumped from the van and grabbed the man from behind. Despite his size, he was no weakling. As he struggled to free himself he said, "I don't care what you do to me, I'm not leaving until I see Steve McQueen."

At that moment Norman, Steve's carpenter, arrived. As much as I wanted to personally haul the little man away, my biggest concern at the moment was Steve's ice cream which I'd left on the hot front seat of my van. If it was to reach Steve before turning to soup, time was critical. "Norman, help Barbara get rid of this guy," I said. "I've got to get back inside." I continued on while Norman took over.

With brown bag in hand, I followed Steve's instructions, sneaking around the back of the house through the yard and up the stairs of the porch that led to his bedroom. I tried the French doors. The knob wouldn't turn; Steve had forgotten to unlock it. I tapped lightly on the glass but he didn't hear me. He was lying in bed, eyes open toward the ceiling. I tapped again, harder. "Open the door," I whispered, "let me in!"

Steve sat up, grinning. Then he was at the door, pulling me inside. He had purposely left the door locked, he admitted, having remembered a mysterious telephone call he'd received only the day before. On hearing Steve's voice the caller had clicked off without saying a word. "Did you remember to bring a plastic spoon?" he asked.

"It's in the bag; napkins and everything."

Steve locked the door again then sat on the edge of his bed and pried off the lid of the carton. His eyes widened as his chocolate-covered sundae came into view. He started to dip in then changed his mind. "Come on," he said, "let's take this into the bathroom where we can be alone."

We moved into the narrow room and shut the door. "Lock it," Steve said, sitting on the lid of the toilet. Then, with tremendous enthusiasm, he began scooping the gooey concoction into his mouth.

I was suddenly swept with guilt. "Are you sure that won't hurt you, Steve? I don't want to throw you off your diet."

"Forget it. Ice cream's good for you. They serve it in hospitals, don't they?"

He was finished almost before he started, repeatedly scraping the carton to salvage every last morsel. Reluctantly, he parted with the empty shell, saying, "Put everything back in the paper bag and stash it where the nurses won't find it. I don't want any evidence around."

"What did the doctors really tell you?"

"When?"

"This morning. What were they doing here?"

"Oh," he said, wiping his mouth, "remember the operation I was telling you about? Well, they wanted to check me out to see if I was strong enough to handle it. I guess I checked out fine. Anyway, I got the green light if I want it. Now it's up to me to make the final decision."

"What do you think you'll do?"

"I don't know," he sighed. "I really don't know." Now that the excitement was over he seemed to be tiring. "Help me back into bed, will you? I guess I've been sitting up too long."

I returned to the house circuitously, passing the trash cans en route. I was hoping to see Barbara for a report on the stranger at the gate, but Annie stopped me just inside the door. "Your wife called," she said. "She sounded like she has something urgent to tell you."

She did. Billy Graham's office had phoned our apartment in Fillmore not knowing that Steve had returned from Mexico. "Reverend Graham has been delayed in Tokyo a few days," Judy said, "but he'll be back on Monday and will call then to arrange a meeting."

I told Steve immediately. "Monday," he repeated, making it sound light-years away. "Well, be sure to let him know I'm here when he calls . . . and ask him to come see me. Find out if he can come right away."

Outside, just beyond the gate, Norman had been unable to discourage the intruder. The two men were engaged in a game of push and shove; neither one appeared to be winning. "He won't leave," Norman said, disgusted. "I march him down to the road and he keeps coming back."

"I won't go until I see Steve McQueen," the little man said stubbornly. "God sent me to pray for him."

I grabbed his arm. "You don't have to see Steve to do that. You can pray for him anywhere."

He collapsed on the driveway, much as a striker would do. "This isn't your property," he said. "You can't make me leave." He was right in that regard. The property outside the gate belonged to the Texaco company.

"Well, maybe the sheriff can," said Norman.

"Call him!" the little man said, defiantly.

It didn't take long for Deputy Dennis to arrive. "You have a choice," he told the intruder, "you can either leave quietly on your own or be arrested and taken to jail. What'll it be?"

The man suddenly became mute. He was handcuffed, put into the deputy's squad car and driven away. With some relief, Norman said, "Well, that's that!"

It wasn't. Several hours later the little man was back again, lurking in the lemon grove near the lower road. Again, the sheriff's office was alerted.

"There's not much we can do," Deputy Dennis admitted on returning. "He hasn't committed a crime so we can't hold him too long. But now that it's getting late, we'll try to keep him overnight—if that's what you'd like."

As long as possible, Norman and I agreed.

As the deputy led the man away, I noticed a length of rope dangling from his back pocket. When questioned about it he said he occasionally wrapped it around his waist much like a belt. It seemed like a strange explanation but there was no way to disprove it.

For someone whose motives were ostensibly good, the little man had managed to create an uneasiness around the ranch. With no guarantees of his confinement overnight, Norman volunteered to spend the evening guarding Steve's property. A small camper was set up near the front gate where Norman took cover.

There were no further incidents that night, but the following morning as I was arriving for work I spotted the familiar shape of the stranger walking along the road leading to the ranch. I continued on to alert Norman. "The guy's back again," I said. "Better call the sheriff's office."

By the time Deputy Dennis arrived, the man was still down by the road but nearing the cutoff to Steve's driveway. Once again he was apprehended. "You can keep doing this but you can't stop me," he said smugly. "I've got to see Steve McQueen. I've got to pray for him."

The deputy took me aside. "The only way we can lock the man up is to get a formal complaint against him," he said. "If you can get somebody from Texaco out here we can book the man for trespassing."

I telephoned the local Texaco office and one of their representatives arrived shortly; he confronted the intruder with the threat of imprisonment if he failed to vacate the company land. Nothing seemed to phase the man. He steadfastly refused to budge.

"I hope you have a good lawyer," the Texaco representative said. With that the man was taken away, never again to be seen along South Mountain Road.

When Steve found out about the incident he became obsessed with the thought that he was a marked man. For some reason he felt very strongly that there would be an attempt on his life. He did not hesitate to talk about his fears but he would do so only in complete privacy. The hot tub, away from the house, afforded that. Besides, the pain in his back had flared up again.

Although Steve was weak, he could now walk the distance from his bed to the edge of the tub without assistance. It was encouraging to see how much stronger he'd become just since his return to Santa Paula.

"Remember that strange phone call I told you about?" he said, slowly easing into the swirling water. "Things like that really frighten me. I keep thinking there might be some crackpots out to get me, people who don't want me to pull through 'cause it might show they've been wrong all along. A lot of so-called experts could get real embarrassed because of me."

A shaft of sunlight streaming through the latticed pool enclosure caught Steve in the eyes. Half sitting, half floating, he worked his way around the tub until his back faced the blinding glare. "I don't have to tell you what I think of Kelley's program," he went on. "I'm for it 100 percent. The man works miracles. But everybody's out to discredit him. Nobody gives the guy credit for *trying*. Nobody'll even admit that he *might* be on the right track. Well, I'd rather give it everything I've got than give up—like the other doctors did with me. 'That's it,' they said. 'Forget it. Drop dead!' And they call themselves *experts*. If they're such experts, why don't they know what to do? They didn't because they were stumped. There've only been about thirty cases of my type of cancer, and those poor people all died. But the good doctors wouldn't recommend trying something new, oh, no. That'd be ridiculous. *It could kill you!* I wonder who's the most scared . . . them or me."

Steve narrowed his eyes. "I have a bad feeling that

some pretty important people don't want me to make it. And if they're desperate enough, well . . . " He cupped his hands and raised them out of the water, watching as the clear liquid slowly drained through his fingers. "Help me out of here," he said suddenly. "The heat seems to have sapped all my strength."

As we walked slowly back toward the house, Steve said, "I've got some heavy decisions to make today . . . and a lot of praying to do." In a quiet voice, he added, "I'd like you to say a little prayer for me tonight."

I told him I would, but he didn't have to ask. Judy and I prayed for Steve every night.

Chapter Thirteen

The call from Billy Graham came on Monday morning, November 3. He was in Los Angeles, he said, and would be for the next few days, staying at the Marriott Hotel near the airport. He wondered if Steve was still interested in seeing him.

The answer, of course, was *yes*. Steve had left definite instructions that he wanted to see Dr. Graham as soon as possible and, if it could be arranged, at the ranch.

I relayed Steve's message. Without hesitating, Dr. Graham made himself immediately available. Not only that, he offered to postpone his plans for the coming days in order to spend as much time as necessary with Steve.

Steve was thrilled with the news. The prospect of seeing Billy Graham at last, having the man at his bedside, brought tears of joy. Steve was in a rare mood anyway, more relaxed than he'd been for months. It was as if a great burden had been lifted during the night. "You'd better be on your way," he said, prodding me on. "We can't keep Billy Graham waiting."

I took the van and headed for the Marriott Hotel in Los Angeles. An hour and a half later I was standing before Room 1101. To my surprise, Dr. Graham answered the door himself. "Come on in," he smiled. "We're just about ready." There were two other men in the room whom he introduced as Bill Brown and T.W. Wilson. Bill Brown, he explained, was the president of World Wide Pictures and a member of the Billy Graham Crusade Team. T.W. Wilson had been associated with Billy Graham since the beginning of his ministry. "Do you think Steve will mind if I wear my blue jeans?" he asked.

"Not at all, Rev. Graham," I answered. "That's what Steve wears."

He smiled again. "You don't have to call me Rev. Graham. Call me Billy."

A few minutes later we were on our way. In order to save me a return trip to Los Angeles, it was decided that Billy would ride with me in the van, with Bill Brown and T.W. Wilson following in another car which would bring them back. Along the way, Billy began to ask questions. He said he had read about Steve's illness and was praying for him both spiritually and physically, but he wanted to know more about Steve's background since moving to Santa Paula. I briefly summarized Steve's activities since then. The most significant was that he had placed his trust in Jesus Christ as his Saviour. He had bought a fifteen-acre ranch near the airport, several airplanes, and had learned to fly. He had also married a beautiful lady named Barbara. Billy seemed interested in the ranch. "I was raised on a ranch myself," he remarked, "in North Carolina."

We drove first to Fillmore. Bill and T.W. would stay

there with Judy while Billy was with Steve.

As Billy Graham remembers: "Grady drove me to the small ranch in Santa Paula that Steve had purchased apparently for privacy purposes. The house was a rather old building and certainly was not ostentatious. It looked like the kind of place where a person could put on his blue jeans and really relax. It was hidden away at the foot of some mountains and was almost inaccessible to any curiosity-minded people."

When we arrived at the ranch, Tina and Annie were scurrying about tossing things into open suitcases. Other pieces of luggage, already packed, were piled near the back door. It looked like an evacuation scene. Cornering Tina and Annie, I asked, "What's going on?"

"We're all leaving for Dallas," Tina said in a rush. "Steve's decided to go ahead with the operation. It's all set for Thursday."

"Where's Barbara?"

"She went on ahead. You know how afraid she is of flying commercial airlines, so she packed and left. Just drove off."

"She *drove* to Dallas?"

"She wanted to get a head start."

"*Alone?*" Everything was suddenly moving too fast. "Where's Steve?" I wanted to know. I was beginning to feel panicky.

"In bed," Tina said.

"Well, there's somebody here he wants to see." Billy Graham stood virtually ignored in the dining room. I hurriedly introduced him.

Tina disappeared momentarily behind Steve's closed door. When she returned I escorted Billy inside. The two men were left alone.

In his own words, Billy Graham remembers that long-awaited meeting with Steve McQueen: "Though I had never met him before I recognized him immediately from his pictures, even though he had lost considerable weight. His eyes were bright and shiny. He sat up in bed and greeted me warmly.

"He told me of his spiritual experience. He said that about three months before he knew he was ill he had accepted Christ as his Saviour and had started going to church, reading his Bible, and praying. He said he had undergone a total transformation of his thinking and his life.

"Apparently he had been led to Christ by a pilot that he had hired to teach him to fly an old vintage airplane. He apparently saw something in this pilot, Sammy Mason, that he admired and liked, and asked what made the difference in his life—and Sammy Mason sat down and carefully explained how Christ had changed his life. Steve later learned that he had a fast-moving and possibly incurable cancer. While this was a shattering blow, his new faith in Christ became his resource for extra strength.

"I sensed during our conversations—interrupted only when the nurses would come to give him shots—that he was happy and totally at peace. He informed me that he was leaving for an undisclosed destination for an operation to remove the last tumor. He said the treatment he had received had removed all the tumors except a rather large one in his stomach—and he pulled up his pajamas and showed me. He said that when he got that removed his chances would be good for recovery, although he admitted, 'I have about a 50 percent chance of surviving the operation.'

"I read him a number of passages of Scripture and prayed with him several times.

"After two hours, I left the room and went out to the kitchen to talk to the nurses, his housekeeper, and Grady Ragsdale. I wanted to give Steve a bit of rest. About an hour later I was informed that he wanted to see me again. We had another time of spiritual discussion, Bible reading and prayer. I was then informed that it was time to go to Ventura County Airport in Oxnard where a private Lear jet was waiting to take him for his operation. He never told me where the operation was to take place. I assumed it was somewhere in Mexico."

Billy Graham waited alone outside Steve's bedroom while Tina, Annie, and I helped ready Steve for the flight. Steve asked if Billy had gone. "No," I said, "he's still here."

"Do you think he'd ride with me to the airport?"

"I'm sure he would," I answered and, indeed, that was Billy Graham's reply.

I brought Steve's wheelchair and helped him in. Then we were on our way, heading slowly through the house toward the back door. His head turned constantly, as if to collect memories that would last 'til his return. In the kitchen, however, Steve asked to stop. "Let me sit here for a minute," he said quietly. He was drawn to the breakfast table. "That's the best place in the house," he smiled. On top of the table sat one of Judy's chocolate cakes. Steve looked at Wilma and said, "I'd like to take that with me." Wilma wrapped the cake and placed it in Steve's lap.

He signaled to move out onto the driveway. He had failed to notice the poem Barbara had taped to one of the kitchen walls that morning before her departure. The poem was a favorite of Barbara's, one she had copied in her own handwriting especially for Steve to see:

> I believe that the birds will stay singing
> And my garden will stay with its green trees,
> With its waterfall.
> Many afternoons the sky will be blue and placid
> And the bells in the belfry will chime

As they are chiming this very afternoon.
The people who have loved me will pass away
And the town will burst anew every year.
But my spirit will always wander nostalgic
In the same recondite corner of my flower gar-
den.

Steve was being transported to the airport in a camper
that contained a bed so that he could recline along the way.
I was the designated driver. Sitting with me up front were
Dr. McKee and Annie. Tina decided to travel the twenty
miles with her husband, Jack, and her mother and her
daughter who had recently joined her in Santa Paula. Billy
Graham was in back, alone with Steve.

Recalling their final, fateful moments together, Dr.
Graham said:

"They had a large comfortable coach to carry Steve
over some rather rough roads to the airport. We talked,
but I could see that he was getting weary so I suggested
that he lie back and rest a few moments. He rested part of
the time, and when he felt he had gained a little strength
he would sit up again and ask more questions.

"The plane was parked at one end of the field, quite a
distance from the small terminal where people might know
what was going on. Steve wanted total privacy because
there had been a great deal of speculation in the press.
Grady pulled the camper as close to the plane as he could,
so there would be less chance of Steve's being seen had
there been reporters in the area.

"Steve got out of the bus and walked, mostly under his
own steam, to the plane where they had two reclining
seats for him to lie partially down. Then he called me again
and asked if I would go on the plane and have another
prayer with him, which I did. It was at that point that I
gave him my Bible and inscribed it to him."

After spending over three hours with Steve, Billy Graham deplaned as the engines fired. I took his place on board. I needed a private moment with Steve; I hadn't been alone with him since he'd made his decision to have the operation.

Steve was buckled in his makeshift bed with tears in his eyes. When he saw me approach he began to smile. It was that familiar grin I'd seen so many times. "Don't worry about me, pal," he said, taking my hand. "You be strong, 'cause I'll be all right."

"I know you will, Steve. Just take care and I'll see you soon. You know that I love you."

"I love you too, Grady," he said. "Be strong. It'll all work out."

The pilot revved the engines. I pulled away quickly and jumped from the plane. As I looked back I could see Steve clutching Billy Graham's Bible. "God bless you, Steve," I cried.

The next thing I knew the hatch was sliding shut and the plane was taxiing down the runway. Then in a burst of power it was airborne, streaking through the sky. All too soon it was gone, obscured by the faraway clouds.

Chapter Fourteen

I returned to Santa Paula alone. Tina, Annie, and Dr. McKee were on the plane with Steve. Tina's family had gone on to Los Angeles where they planned to board a commercial flight that would reunite them with Tina in Dallas. Billy Graham was not anxious to return to his hotel by car. He was in a pensive mood and the thought of a long quiet drive held little appeal. A commuter jet to Los Angeles was boarding near the terminal. He purchased a ticket then alerted his associates that he would not be accompanying them.

Billy Graham later reflected: "I look back on that experience with Steve with thanksgiving and some amazement. I had planned to minister to him but, as a matter of fact, he had ministered to me. His cheerfulness, his bright eyes, his excitement about his relationship to God will never be forgotten."

I tried to carry some of that thinking home with me. But it was nearly impossible to stay in a positive frame of mind. I worried constantly not only about Steve's health but his safety. Judy's deep faith and compassion nourished me through the daylight hours. At night, however, alone at the ranch and surrounded by memories, sleep wouldn't come.

I longed to hear from Barbara and never strayed far from the telephone. It did not ring. Radio and television carried no reports from Dallas. Newspapers failed to alert their readers to the status of Steve's condition. After months of headlines, his name was strangely inconspicuous.

By Wednesday afternoon on November 5, with the operation less than twenty-four hours away, I could no longer sit still. "I've got to know what's going on," I told Judy frantically. "I've got to go to Dallas." Where I would go once I reached the city, I didn't know. But I was determined to find Steve.

"I understand," Judy said. "You should be there." She was totally supportive. She even offered to drive me to the airport in Los Angeles and, in my absence, stay at the ranch.

I was on the phone to Steve's office immediately. "I'm going to Dallas," I told his secretary. "Make arrangements with the bank in Santa Paula to have funds available for my travel expenses."

Less than thirty minutes later she called back. She had spoken with the bank, she said; the money was waiting to be picked up. But in the short time since I'd last spoken with her there had been other developments. She had received a hurried call from Barbara. "Send Grady," Barbara had said, "he's family." A ticket was on hold at the United Airlines counter for a flight leaving at 7:00 P.M.

I quickly threw a few things into a suitcase, raced to

the bank, met Judy in Fillmore and we were on our way to
Los Angeles. With the late start and the rush hour freeway traffic we began to wonder whether we'd reach the
airport in time. We did, but just barely. I kissed Judy goodbye, and no sooner did I board the plane than the door
slammed shut behind me. In the rush I was able only to
verify the flight number. It wasn't until the plane was airborne that I discovered its destination was not Dallas but
El Paso. My heart sank. Had I boarded the wrong plane? I
wondered. If so, there was nothing to do now but ride it
out. In El Paso I would catch the next flight to Dallas.

On landing, I headed first for the luggage claim area. It
was there I spotted a friendly face—Tina's husband Jack.
He was supposed to be in Dallas too! "What are you doing
here?" I asked, confused.

He laughed, then calmly said, "I'm here to meet you."

"But how did you know I'd be landing *here*?"

"Dallas was only a decoy," he explained. "Steve
wanted it that way. He's just across the border in Juarez."

Jack walked me to his car and we drove several miles
along darkened streets until we reached a deserted parking lot behind an old brick building. On a hillside not too far
away a large lighted star blazed against the night sky. For
me, at least, it became a symbol of hope.

"This is it," Jack said suddenly, "we're here."

What "here" meant, I didn't know. From the outside,
the building had an uninviting look. It could have been a
garage or an old warehouse. As it turned out, we had
reached the Santa Rosa Clinic.

The front door was locked. A small male Mexican
finally answered Jack's repeated knocks. He was dressed
in white and identified himself as one of the technicians.
He recognized Jack and let us in, then relocked the door.
"Wait there," Jack said, pointing to a laboratory room.
Then he disappeared. He was back in a moment shaking

his head. "I thought you might be able to see Steve tonight," he said, "but Tina tells me he's asleep. Don't worry, he's doing fine. Dr. McKee's with him 'round the clock." Jack smiled faintly then took my arm. "Come on, we'll go to the motel. Barbara's reserved a room for you."

The Las Fuentes Motel in Juarez was like a glittering oasis in the darkness, a jewel amid the squalor. Comfortable and clean, it was a welcome sight.

We made our way through the lobby. "Is Barbara staying here too?" I wanted to know.

"We all are," he nodded. "It's close to the clinic."

I was standing at the registration desk when I heard my name being paged. Barbara was on the house phone. "Just checking to see if you made it," she said, sounding cheery. But she soon admitted that she was bone tired. She'd had a long, strenuous day and, as she was facing more of the same, she was heading for bed. "I'll see you first thing in the morning," she said finally. "We'll go to the clinic together."

On Thursday, early, we met for coffee then drove the short distance to the old brick building. In daylight it seemed no more impressive nor inspired more confidence than it had the night before. Barbara had talked of seeing Steve prior to his surgery. We soon learned, however, that that would be impossible. We had arrived too late; he was already being prepped for the operation.

Tina made the disappointment bearable. She found us standing forlornly in the hallway outside Steve's room; her smiling face was like a ray of sunshine. "Things couldn't be going better," she said brightly. "Steve's spirits are so high. He's even kept his sense of humor."

Indeed, Steve appeared ready for battle. For the moment, at least, the tension had been relieved.

Over the next several crucial hours, Barbara was rarely left uninformed. Tina and Annie, like relay runners, appeared at intervals to feed her bits of news regarding Steve's progress and the various procedures involved in the delicate operation. She knew when Steve was sedated and that the last-minute examination by Dr. Santos Vargas showed his heart to be strong. She learned when the small tumor in Steve's neck was removed and when they began working to excise the larger one in his stomach. At one point, Dr. Kelley appeared to say that several other patients under his care had traveled great distances to donate blood for Steve. That was extremely important, he felt, as they had built up immunities applicable to Steve's program. Dr. Kelley seemed highly pleased with the way the surgery was progressing.

When at last the large tumor was completely removed, Annie advised, "Steve's doing beautifully." She had been given permission to invite Barbara and me to watch the suturing, in progress, through the window of the operating room.

Barbara paled at the thought. "Oh, no," she said, turning away. "I'll wait a little while. As long as he's doing fine."

"He is fine," Annie smiled, emphasizing each word.

I could not resist the invitation. I followed Annie to the viewing area adjoining the small operating room. Through the window I could see Steve. He was lying on his back under a brilliant light, an oxygen mask covering his face. Dr. Santos Vargas was methodically working over him. On a nearby table, in a tray, lay a fleshy substance the size of a baseball. I stood half frozen, staring in disbelief. Nothing, at the moment, seemed real.

I left quickly and rejoined Barbara. She was sitting nervously in a waiting area down the hall. Shortly, the doors of the operating room opened wide and Steve was wheeled out on a gurney. An IV bottle dangled overhead from a moveable stand; a single line ran into his arm.

The gurney, flanked by a small army of white-coated attendants, passed directly by us on its way to the recovery room. Steve's eyes were partially open, unfocused and staring; he was still under the effects of the anesthesia. Dr. Santos Vargas followed closely behind. The strain of the operation showed clearly on his face as he signaled to Barbara that he would join her momentarily. Barbara seemed desperate to talk with the surgeon. She would not relax until she had received official word on Steve's condition.

When Dr. Santos Vargas returned, still in his surgical garb, the strain that was so noticeable only a short time earlier had dissipated. Now, he appeared at ease, almost jovial as he reported that Steve was doing extremely well. He made a special point of saying that Steve's heart was "going strong."

Barbara sighed with some relief, but there were questions to be answered. Dr. Santos Vargas led her into a small room across the way, then closed the door. Through the large window that opened onto the waiting area I could see them talking. From time to time the surgeon held up a series of x-rays for Barbara to study. They were together for nearly fifteen minutes.

Barbara was smiling when she left the meeting. "The doctor's really pleased with the way things have gone so far," she said. "It looks like Steve's going to be fine. She made an expression that seemed to say, "Please, dear God, stay with my husband. Please make him well again."

It wasn't long before Tina was bringing more encouraging news. As Steve regained consciousness, his first words were, "Is my stomach flat now?" It was a good sign, everyone agreed. Steve was less concerned about the success of the operation than his appearance. He hadn't lost his competitive determination.

"When can I see him?" Barbara asked.

Tina didn't waste words. "Now," she said quickly. "He's been asking for you."

Barbara wasn't allowed to stay very long, just time enough to see for herself what everyone had been saying: Steve had truly come through the operation with flying colors! And while she had hoped to remain longer by his side, she understood when Tina signaled that Steve needed rest. That, without question, was most important now. Besides, there would be opportunities to be together later. Many more. A lifetime.

For the first time that day, Barbara thought of food. Earlier, we had been too rushed to stop for breakfast. The subject hadn't even come up we were so intent on reaching the clinic. Now, with Steve resting comfortably and her mind more at ease, it held some interest. We found a small cafe near the motel and enjoyed a somewhat leisurely meal. Understandably, Barbara did not feel completely at ease being away from Steve for too long.

Steve was still sleeping when we returned to the clinic. Dr. McKee kept a close watch on him, checking his vital signs periodically. Steve was never unattended. Whenever Dr. McKee left his side, Annie or Tina would replace him.

Occasionally, Steve would awaken for brief periods and Barbara would be called in to visit. She would stay only until he drifted off again. Her reports of those times together were always the same: "He's in very good spirits but still weak and tired." And, always, she was so pleased to know that Steve was progressing so beautifully.

It was late afternoon when Dr. McKee reported that Steve had been heavily sedated and would probably sleep through the night. He advised Barbara to get some rest and return in the morning. Tina and Annie agreed; it would be senseless to stay. For now, there was nothing more to do.

The long ordeal and the frightening worrisome events of the day had taken their toll on Barbara. And, now, with the realization that the worst was over, she appeared drained. For nearly a year she had lived with the fear of Steve's illness. She had been strong, not for herself but for Steve. She had worked unstintingly under the most extreme conditions, stress and strain, never once complaining. She was never even heard to say, "I'm tired." Happily, all that had changed. She had only to sit by and wait. And pray.

As we made our way back to the motel, however, it became fairly obvious that Barbara needed some reassuring. Without that, at times like this, the mind can start playing tricks. There was only one person who could truly be of help to her. "Would you like me to call Billy Graham?" I suggested. "Would you like to talk to him?"

At first, Barbara looked at me rather strangely, as if the idea was utterly ridiculous. I half expected her to say, "You can't call him at the drop of a hat . . . just to talk." But she didn't. She thought for a moment, then said, "I think I do need to talk with him. Yes, go ahead. Call him— please."

I immediately telephoned the evangelist's office in Burbank, California and left a message for him to return the call as soon as possible. The phone rang within the hour. "I just got word you wanted to speak with me," Billy Graham said. He had been thinking of Steve, and hoped someone would contact him with word of Steve's progress.

I told Billy how well the operation had gone. He received the news with great joy, adding, "Be sure to tell Steve that I'll be praying for him."

I assured him that I would, then handed the receiver to Barbara and left the room. I returned not too many minutes later with my hands full. Barbara had finished her conversation. "Where have you been?" she asked.

"Here's your dinner," I said, offering her a paper bag. "I thought you might be hungry."

She sighed, "I don't even know what time it is."

"It's getting late, and you'd better eat something."

She poked around in the bag and pulled out a hamburger. "This looks good," she smiled. "Where did you have to go?"

"Downstairs," I said, "there's a coffee shop."

Barbara took a small bite, then another. Before long she was eating with enthusiasm. She said nothing about her brief talk with Billy Graham. She spoke only about Steve, of miracles and hope. But in the short time since our return from the clinic, Barbara had changed. Now there was a sureness in her voice, and her eyes reflected an inner peace. I left her that evening, certain that her newfound strength would sustain her through the night.

The telephone in my room rang at 4:10 A.M., awakening me from a deep sleep. I picked up the receiver and, for several seconds, no one answered. It was as if the person on the other end was afraid to speak, to say the words that had to be said. A shudder ran through my body as I realized who the caller was. It had to be Barbara. "I have some bad news," she said finally, her voice breaking. "Steve passed away twenty minutes ago."

Chapter Fifteen

I raced down the hallway to Barbara's room, praying with every step that there was some mistake. She's wrong, I told myself, *she has to be wrong*! But the moment I saw her I knew it was true. She was seated on her bed, unmoving, staring hopelessly into space.

"How . . . why?" I stammered, sitting beside her.

For a long moment, she didn't answer. Only a stony silence filled the room which hours earlier had known such hope, so many expectations. Now it seemed so empty. "It was his heart," she said, barely audible, at last. She spoke in a monotone, her eyes still gazing blankly. "He just wasn't strong enough."

It wasn't long before Dr. McKee and Annie arrived from the clinic. They appeared devastated. Steve's death had affected them deeply. They had lost more than a patient. They had lost a friend.

Dr. McKee confirmed that Steve had had a heart attack, his weakened body ultimately unable to endure the strain of surgery. "What a tragedy," he said. "Steve fought so hard, and came so close." He closed his eyes as he said, "But we failed."

Barbara and the doctor agreed that news of Steve's passing should not be released until his body was returned to California. They feared an onrush not only from the press but also the curious. It was also decided that Barbara and Annie would fly home immediately, if possible, aboard a chartered jet. A separate charter flight, to leave as soon as preparations were completed, would carry Steve. "I'd like you to fly with him, Grady," Barbara said, " . . . if you will. I think Steve would want that."

If I will? To fly with Steve on his final flight would be an honor.

Once details were finalized, Barbara and Annie began packing. Now Dr. McKee talked of returning to the clinic; there were papers to sign and permits to obtain before Steve could leave Mexico. I volunteered to drive him. The offer was purely selfish. In my mind and heart there lingered doubts about Steve's death. To satisfy those feelings I had to see Steve one last time.

It was nearly 7:00 A.M. when we arrived at the clinic. There was an eerie quiet about the place and a noticeable absence of people. Where were all the attendants? I wondered. Where were the other patients? Perhaps the hour had something to do with it, but I had an uneasy feeling that we had entered an abandoned building. Or that the others were behind locked doors, afraid to be seen.

Dr. McKee led me down a long hallway, past the darkened operating room that only yesterday was ablaze with light and hope, to a smaller room. As he opened the door I saw Tina. She was standing beside a bed, her normally erect posture slumped in defeat. We looked at each other and said nothing. She turned slowly toward the bed then back again. She was near tears.

My feet were rooted to the floor. I wanted to step inside that room but something was holding me back. Perhaps I didn't really want to know the truth. Or face it.

Tina reached out. Slowly I began to move forward, and as I drew closer I could see Steve. His eyes were now bright and clear—bluer than I'd ever seen them. They still had that familiar twinkle and were no longer clouded with fear and uncertainty. His expression was so peaceful he seemed to be saying, "Don't cry for me, pal. I've left this ill body and now I'm in heaven." My mind was at last freed of doubts. Steve had reached the doors of heaven and they had opened to him.

I pulled the bed covering slightly aside to grasp Steve's hand one last time. It was then that I saw the Bible Billy Graham had given to him. Steve was still holding it.

"There's something you should see," Dr. McKee said. He escorted me from the room to one of the offices and pulled a folder from the file. Inside was a set of Steve's x-rays. One, he said, had been taken at the Plaza Santa Maria in July shortly after Steve's arrival, the other just before his departure in October. "The white area is the cancer," he explained, holding the x-rays against a lighted viewing panel. "As you can see, we almost had it beaten."

To my untrained eyes, the diseased areas appeared to have been noticeably reduced over the three-month period. The comparison was rather startling.

"Steve put up a gallant fight," Dr. McKee said in a baleful tone. "He came so close to winning." He set the negatives aside and went to the telephone. "Well, if I'm going to get those legal permits I'd better get busy."

I left the clinic in search of something cold to drink. Not far away, a vendor was opening his doors to the day's tourist trade. Inside, a small radio was playing a lively Mexican tune. As I was making my purchase, the music was suddenly interrupted by a news bulletin. "We have just received a report," the announcer began, "that American film star Steve McQueen . . . " I didn't wait to hear more. Dr. McKee and Tina had to be alerted. It would only be a matter of minutes until the area was swarming with reporters.

When I reached the clinic, the waiting area was already beginning to crowd with members of the press. They stood pacing, desperate for someone to appear to answer their questions. Unknowingly, I walked into their midst. At once, I was surrounded by microphones. "Were you a relative of McQueen's?" they wanted to know. "A friend? What's your connection here? What can you tell us?" The questions came nonstop.

I held up my hands in mock surrender. "I don't know anything about it," I said. "I'm here to see someone else." They backed off as if I'd suddenly become contagious; I quickly disappeared in search of Tina.

She was in one of the back offices. "We've got to hurry," I told her. "The word's out."

"Dr. McKee's still trying to make arrangements to move Steve," she said rather helplessly, "and he's having some problems with the permits. It could be a while."

It didn't take as long as long as anticipated. Once the clearances were obtained, the plan became relatively simple. Tina and I were to go directly to the mortuary (Funerales Santa Rosa) in Juarez, where Steve was to be prepared for transportation, while Dr. McKee and several attendants from the clinic followed in a separate vehicle with Steve's body.

As Tina and I slipped through a back door she was seen—and recognized—by one of the reporters. We were off, speeding along the dusty alleyway before he could give chase. We stopped at the motel, hastily packed, then took a circuitous route down side roads to the mortuary and parked in a sheltered area several hundred yards away.

It was nearly two hours before Dr. McKee appeared. He was standing at the alley entrance to the mortuary scanning the narrow roadway. I pulled forward to meet him. "It won't be much longer," he said. "Why don't you two start for the airport now? I'll wait and ride with Steve in the station wagon. We'll be along in a few minutes."

It was good to be on our way, moving toward the El Paso airport and home. My biggest concern now was the plane. It had been standing by since early morning when the arrangements were first made. At least, I hoped it was still standing by.

The road leading to the border was jammed with tourists; the drive seemed endless. Even after we crossed into the United States we were unable to pick up much time. Just outside the airport, Tina spotted a young boy hawking newspapers from a corner stand. We were moving so slowly it was easy to read the huge headlines: STEVE MCQUEEN DIES IN JUAREZ.

Tina's husband, Jack, was waiting anxiously at the airport terminal. He had been there for some time, not knowing exactly when we would arrive. Everything was ready to go, he said; he had been talking with the men who would be piloting our charter flight. He also learned that arrangements had been made to allow the people from the mortuary to drive up directly to the plane so Steve could be boarded quickly.

For nearly an hour, the three of us craned our necks by the window that overlooked the security gate. Then a station wagon appeared. Within seconds, flashbulbs began popping and the vehicle was surrounded. We ran from the terminal to the plane as the gate slowly opened and the wagon sped through. As the gate closed the guards were unable to stop the onrush of reporters, photographers, and fans. Some squeezed through the narrowing gap, others climbed fences and barricades. The approach to the plane suddenly became a mass of humanity as gawking strangers closed in from every direction in a desperate attempt to view the transfer of the body. Cameras clicked constantly to record the macabre scene.

By the time Jack, Tina, and I reached the station wagon, Dr. McKee and the pilots were loading the casket aboard the plane. As we stopped to help, one of the attendants from the mortuary pulled out a camera and began taking pictures at close range. Dr. McKee was the first to see him and he ordered the man to stop. Either the attendant couldn't hear in the confusion or he didn't want to; he steadily moved closer and continued shooting.

Something inside me snapped. I could think only of Steve and his need for privacy. He had an almost phobic aversion to cameras in his personal life. "Give me the camera," I demanded, confronting the attendant.

He stepped around me to get another shot.

"I want the film," I said. "Give me the camera or I'll break it."

The attendant smiled in an ugly way, refocused and took another picture. It wasn't until Dr. McKee and Jack joined me that he knew we were serious. Reluctantly, he opened his camera and pulled out the film.

Tina called us to board; the pilots were readying for takeoff. Then we were in our seats and the jet was streaking down the runway. As I looked back, I could see a cluster of photographers racing behind on foot—still shooting pictures.

The skies over Ventura County were thick with coastal clouds and fog. The flight home took less than ninety minutes even though we did not land as scheduled. The poor

visibility had nothing to do with it. Soon after departing El
Paso I had asked one of the pilots if it would be possible to
fly over Steve's ranch before landing at the airport, which
meant slightly altering our final approach. "Sure," he said,
without questioning the request, "I think your boss would
like that."

Now, as the pilots prepared the plane for landing, Tina
sat quietly staring into space. She appeared lost in
thought. Only four days earlier she had taken off from this
very same place, filled with such high hopes and expectations. Four days. It seemed an eternity.

Dense fog swirled about the runway as the plane
touched down; it was so thick that seeing past the wing
tips was impossible. That was of less concern, however,
than the possibility of what awaited at the terminal. The
near riot in El Paso put everyone on guard. No one quite
knew what to expect.

As a precaution, the pilots pulled the plane off the runway to the far side of the control tower. As we taxied to a
stop, a long black limousine came into view. When it was
directly beside the plane several men in black appeared.
They were to take Steve to the mortuary in Ventura for
cremation.

Dr. McKee, Tina, Jack, and I took a taxi from the airport to the ranch where Barbara and Annie were waiting.
It was good to be back among familiar surroundings again,
only now the atmosphere was different—strangely inac-
tive and quiet. Barbara wandered aimlessly about, seemingly without purpose or direction. But she was not alone.
She was among people she had come to know and trust
over the past months. And they would be with her through
the night. Knowing that, I continued on to Fillmore and my
family.

On Sunday, November 9, a private memorial service
was held for Steve on the grassy sweep of lawn beside the

pond at the ranch. At Barbara's request only a few close friends were in attendance.

Pastor Leonard DeWitt of the Ventura Missionary Church conducted the service. As he recalls:

"I was able to share several passages of Scripture that had become special to Steve. One verse that meant much to him was John 3:16, 'For God so loved the world that He gave His only begotten Son, that whosoever believeth in Him should not perish, but have everlasting life.'

"Another passage we shared was the wonderful Twenty-third Psalm. In this psalm we read of the great care and provision that the Shepherd gives to His sheep. It is a picture of loving care and provision for every area of life that Christ our Shepherd offers us. That psalm ends with, 'Surely goodness and mercy shall follow me all the days of my life and I shall dwell in the house of the Lord forever.' "

Pastor DeWitt closed the memorial service with a verse. It was from a letter that had been written by an American soldier killed in Viet Nam to two friends back home. The letter was found on the soldier shortly after his death and subsequently mailed.

Pastor DeWitt read the young man's words:

Dear God, I've never spoken to you,
But now I desperately want to know you, too.
You see, God, they told me you didn't exist,
And I, like a fool, believed all this.

Last night from a shell hole I saw your sky;
I figured right then they'd told me a lie.

Had I taken time to see things you had made
I'd have known they weren't calling a spade a spade.

I wonder, God, if you'd take my hand;
Somehow I feel that you understand.
Strange I had to come to this hellish place
Before I had time to see your face.

Well, I guess there isn't much more to say,
But I'm sure glad, Lord, you opened the way.
I guess zero hour will soon be here,
But I'm not afraid since I know you are near.

The signal! Well, God, I guess I'll have to go.
I love you, Lord—this I want you to know.
Look now, this will be a horrible fight!
Who knows, I may come to your house tonight.

Though I wasn't friends with you before,
I wonder, Christ, if you'd wait at your door?
Look, I'm crying—me shedding tears!
How I wish I'd known you these many years.

Well, I have to go now, God. Goodbye.
Strange, since I met you I'm not scared to die.

Source unknown

As the final words were spoken, a hush settled over the small gathering. The silence was short-lived, broken by the roar of oncoming planes. They approached from the east, flying in perfect cross formation. Two of the planes were easily recognizable—they were Steve's, and they flew at the outer tips of the cross. The formation passed directly overhead then slowly faded along the western horizon.

The tribute had been arranged as "a farewell to a

friend who loved to fly." Participating were many of
Steve's comrades from Santa Paula Airport, including
Mike Dewey, Clete Roberts, Doug Dullenkopf, Chuck
Sisto, Perry Schreffler and Pete Mason and Chuck Bail.

It wasn't much later that Bud Ekins, one of Steve's
close friends from his early movie days, was found wandering about the ranch. Bud had covered the years with
Steve; they had shared tough and smooth times along the
way. And dreams.

Now as Bud's eyes canvased Steve's private pocket in
time, his gentle corner of the world seemingly untouched
by progress, Bud nodded approvingly and said, "It took
him a little while but he finally made it. He finally got it all
together."

Epilogue

On November 10, 1980, the day after the memorial service, Barbara left Santa Paula for her cabin in Idaho, accompanied by Annie.

Five days later, Sammy and Pete Mason departed Santa Paula Airport in Steve's yellow Stearman biplane. Their flight took them over the Pacific Ocean, several miles off the coastline, where they scattered Steve's ashes.

The following Monday, I left for Idaho with six cats and a dog. They were Barbara's favorites. She had expressed concern for them and wanted the pets with her in her new home. I remained there nearly a week to help settle the ranch, then proceeded on to El Paso. Barbara had left her car at the airport that fateful Friday morning when she hurriedly returned to Santa Paula. It was evening when I

arrived in the Texas town and, across the way on that
Juarez hillside, the star still burned brightly.

I dream of Steve every now and then, and in the
dreams he always looks healthy. Maybe it's God's way of
letting me know Steve's alright.

Now, on a hilltop above Steve's ranch in Santa Paula,
stands a towering white cross. Near its base an engraved
copper plaque reads:

IN
LOVING MEMORY
OF
MY DEAR FRIEND
STEVE MC QUEEN
1930-1980
GOD BLESS HIM
Grady Ragsdale, Junior